Fondly Dedicated

to

Women and their Families
who are, have been, and will be
On The Move

They Only Laughed Later

Tales of Women on the Move

Edited by
Carol Allen
and
Richard Hill

A Division of Europublic SA/NV

Published by Europublications, Division of Europublic SA/NV,
Avenue Winston Churchill 11 (box 21), B-1180 Brussels.
Tel: + 32 2 343 77 26, Fax: + 32 2 343 93 30.
E-mail: kminke@europublic.com

URL Internet: http://www.understanding-europe.com

Cover design and illustrations: Caroline Ardies

Printed in Belgium. Edition & Imprimerie, Brussels.
D/1997/6421/1   ISBN 90-74440-12-6

Contents

Introduction

Speaking to a group of expatriate women in Madrid, I asked, "What careers have some of you left behind?" One woman immediately blurted out, "My career is moving. Every three years I pack up my family and move." Laughter erupted in the room.

Thank goodness we can laugh! One woman wrote me during the compilation of this anthology, "The reason there isn't *anything* funny written about the life of the expat is because there isn't anything funny about it!" Her essay, however, is in this book.

In 1990, a nonprofit cultural and educational institute in Paris (WICE) organized a conference for expatriate women. It was called Women On The Move and attracted 400 conferees representing twenty-one countries of residence and nineteen different nationalities. It ran for two jam-packed days. The themes of the conference were (1) the woman and her personal identity; (2) the woman and her family; (3) the woman and her career; and (4) general cross-cultural adaptation.

Speakers from Europe, the United States and Canada donated their time to address their areas of expertise. A tingling excitement swept the halls of the Palais de Congrès, home of the conference. The unexpected meeting of old friends from former postings, the networking across country and nationality lines, and most of all, the easing of frustrations and unhappiness into hope were the prevailing highpoints of the two days. One conferee wrote on her evaluation form, "Thank you, thank you, thank you. You have saved my marriage."

Obviously an idea had found its niche. Three other Women on the Move Conferences followed in Brussels and London, and a fifth is planned for Paris.*

The result of these several years of attention to the lives of expatriates, and particularly to women, has resulted in this anthology of humorous essays and anecdotes. While there may seem precious little to laugh about in the midst of all this mobility, the truth is hilarity lurks in the corners of most moves. For our sanity, we must recognize and acknowledge it when it occurs.

This is an important book for mobile women to read and to share with their families; families that accompany them on moves, and families and loved ones who are left behind. Readers will recognize themselves and situations they, too, have experienced.

Human resource personnel, relocation specialists and corporate CEO's should benefit from reading "They Only Laughed Later." They will be inspired and reassured by the women who do more than cope in their roles as global nomads. These women view living abroad as an enriching experience. They set about building stable environments for their families and themselves in otherwise topsy-turvy worlds. They are not defeated by the feeling that they just landed on Mars, that everyone speaks and acts differently than they did "back home," and that their good friend the telephone has just become their worst enemy. (Who knows how to use it? What to say when it rings?)

---

* Women on the Move, sponsored by WICE, Paris - November 1990
Women on the Move, sponsored by FOCUS Career Services, Brussels - March 1992
On the Move, sponsored by FOCUS Information Services, London - Nov. 1993
Women on the Move, sponsored by FOCUS Career Services, Brussels - March 1996
Women on the Move, sponsored by WICE, Paris - March 1998

The essays in this collection are about women. Some essays are about personal identity (or the lack thereof), and some involve family capers. Most illustrate how cultural differences in the host country turn the life of an expat wrongside-out. Few are about careers. Unless a woman is moving abroad *for* her career, she is unlikely to be employable in her new home.

Readers will find stories based on language misunderstandings like Drusilla Walsh's lost cat in Iran and Patsy Souza's haircut in Kuwait.

Differences in local customs and customs back home are humorously described by Tara McKelvy writing about something so banal as trash disposal in Warsaw. Pat Duffy and her husband chuckle their way through birthday parties in Nanjing.

Life's major events take on new meaning in a different culture. Elizabeth Joseph-Mosely describes getting married in Paris and Susan Reynolds Baime has her first child in Barbados, but Sarah Colton goes further. Married to a foreigner, living in a foreign country and raising a bi-lingual, bi-cultural family has clearly provoked funny moments in her life. For this collection she has chosen to describe an annual family trip to the country.

Going home can be just about as jarring as moving to Katmandu. Elizabeth Weir is befuddled on her return to London. Had *everything* changed? And Susan Tiberghien becomes thoroughly confused with the choice of "plastic or paper" in her native USA.

General frustration is gleefully described by Erzsi Deak as she navigates a fourteen-month-old through a Parisian grocery store. Similar frustration almost ruins a cultural outing for Camilla Lee and her husband in Tokyo.

For the weary role of *expat cum tour guide*, Sandra Reid describes her mother's "first - and ONLY - visit" to see her during her five years abroad. In "Exit is the Object," Susan Rose uses a board game to ironically summarize much of the stress of living abroad. The reader smiles and nods knowingly all the way through.

There are others - wet pastries in Germany, homesickness in Istanbul, dirt in Africa, rain in London, dancing class in Paris, a marriage proposal in Uganda... they are funny, and they are encouraging.

"They Only Laughed Later" is a pat-on-the-back and a keep-up-the-good-spirit to all the women who have made and are making the most of living abroad. It is a gentle prod, an out-stretched hand, a go-for-it to those who find coping abroad scary and insurmountable.

Acknowledgements

Who knows what one will receive when one launches a call for manuscripts? For me it was like receiving over 200 presents in the mail over a period of three months. I regret that every single submission could not be reprinted. Funny or not, related to my themes or not, every essay was a story worth telling. First and foremost I acknowledge with gratitude all of the women who willingly shared their stories with me.

My personal appreciation and admiration go to the WICE Board of Directors (1989-90) for going way out on a limb to sponsor the first Women on the Move Conference. Their vision, support and enthusiasm launched a movement of its own, and this anthology is one small piece of that movement.

Longtime friend and colleague Pam Perraud deserves a special thanks. A woman on the move herself, she manages to unfailingly come through with good advice and brilliant ideas, both when she lived in Paris, and now as she lives in New York. Most importantly, Pam makes others laugh.

Ginger Irvine, London, and Barbara Lau, Garmisch, Germany, are steady, dedicated advisors and champions for the successful adaptation of women, families and individuals in our mobile world. They are my good friends and colleagues. I thank them for their support and their leads to people who contributed to the success of this book.

Having undertaken this project as a volunteer, I am grateful to Europublic who believed in this book, saw a need for it and guided me through to its final publication.

Jean Hicks assumed the major task of transferring all the essays on paper, in various formats, to a final disk for our publisher. Jean deserves thanks from all of us.

I am grateful to all of you who are crossing borders, sharing your cultures, making our world a smaller and better place. You are the strongest diplomatic corps any country could have. If you can laugh at yourself and at the folly that follows you from post to post, you will have more than done your part.

Finally, to those among you whose experiences are recounted in this book, thank you. You inspire us all.

Carol Allen

Paris, France
September 1997

On The Move is an international non-profit organization that evolved from the early leadership of the Women on the Move Conferences. OTM is currently affiliated with WICE, a non-profit educational and cultural institute serving the English-speaking community of Paris. Other projects of OTM are a web-site that provides an international data base of services and resources for expatriates all over the world, as well as the publication of a guide book for establishing non-profit organizations abroad, and a career guide book for women whose careers are interrupted by moves abroad.

I consider myself fortunate to have had the opportunity to collaborate, even in a very modest way, on this project.

Some years ago I wrote a book about the European cultures and realised - after I had written it - that, unconsciously, in almost all cases my role models had been men. I prefer to think that this had less to do with male chauvinism than with the simple fact that women show less need to assert their identities.

I have since become increasingly aware that there is a community of women worldwide which transcends frontiers more constructively, and less self-consciously, than most male-inspired organizations.

When I discuss this with audiences, the suggestion comes up that women from all cultures share the same god-given identity as child-rearers and homemakers, and this creates a sense of community which suppresses any petty nationalistic or not-invented-here impulses (this sounds like male chauvinist talk too, but it actually comes from the distaff side of my audiences).

In my experience, women behave a lot better interculturally than men, whatever the reasons may be. Their resilience is well exemplified by the responses to the personal challenges described in this book.

Richard Hill

Brussels, Belgium
September 1997

Shock Therapy

Melanie Billings-Yun

Culture Shock? Never, I sneered. That was for the naïve. I was educated, had studied abroad. I was prepared, I had read every book I could get my hands on about the country we were moving to. I was even seasoned by seven years of cross-cultural marriage. As I think back on it now, twelve years of recurring culture shock later, I marvel at how amazingly naïve I was.

It's not as if I hadn't just been taught a painful lesson in hubris. I will never forget sitting in my publisher's office, seven months pregnant, scoffing at his suggestion that now might not be the best time to take on a new book contract. Heaving my back as straight as I could under the conditions, I intoned with the authority of someone who had read all the latest literature on the subject, "I take it that you are not aware that newborn babies sleep 16-18 hours a day." That memorable gem was uttered only six months before my husband joined the Foreign Service. Maybe it was all those sleepless days and nights that had kept me from getting any wiser.

The truly amazing thing is that, five countries later, I am still as unable to anticipate culture shock as I was incapable of predicting that I was about to give birth to "The Screamer." To be fair, it wouldn't be much of a shock if you could predict it. Still, you would think it wouldn't come as a bolt from the blue, so to speak, every single time. I guess it's the same for all constants in life: I'm sure death, like my tax bill, will come as a big surprise too.

My way of coping with the unavoidable has been to get it over with as quickly as possible. At the Foreign Service Institute they taught us that culture shock was a 6-month process, from excitement, through loss and dislocation, to acceptance. Forget that! I'd already been through six months in hell, with The Screamer in one ear and a deadline-fixated editor in the other. If I have to go through culture shock, my subconscious figured, I want the condensed version. From the very beginning the pattern was set: I'm jolted off my feet and into hysterics on the first or second day in a new country, then safely up and running by the third. After that, there might be little rebouts, but I can usually remain standing.

Hong Kong was our first overseas assignment. What luck: great post, beautiful scenery, fabulous food, exotic yet western-ized. It was the perfect first tour. Stepping out of our hotel into the warm air our first morning (it had been snowing when we left the U.S.), I thought I was in paradise. "Look at that view!" I gushed to my husband, flushed with pride over the wisdom of his choice to uproot our family and see the world. "Look at that sparkling water!" "Look at those charming alleyways!" Then, in a wholly different, strangled voice, "Look at all those people!" ... I had never seen so many people in my life and I mean if you added up everyone I'd seen until that moment.

After a day of hysterics, I had pretty much convinced my hus-band that moving abroad had been the mistake of his life. He came home looking miserable. "This isn't working," he said. "I'm going to quit the Foreign Service and we can move back to the States." And with those magic words I was cured. This was not forever, nor was it a prison. We could go home whenever we wanted. "Oh, really, you don't have to get so dramatic. We just got here," I pronounced, rolling my eyes and sending my husband into his second spin of the day. Since then he's learned: I get culture shock and he gets marital shock. It's only fair.

I never did get wholly used to the crowds in Hong Kong. But after that initial shock, overcrowding felt more like the rain in my hometown, Portland: you may not like it, but it hardly was a sur-prise. I came to accept stoically the inevitable fact that the first person on the elevator would immediately hit the "door close" button in a futile attempt to have the space to himself, so that the door slammed back and forth onto the rest of us as we fought our way on after him. Burdened down with a baby, I learned quickly that I had to fight off swifter folk from slipping in front of me once the taxi door opened (I bought the biggest, toughest stroller on the market and would whack perpetrators in the ankles, exclaiming apologetically, "Oh, I'm so sorry! It never entered my mind that you were about to get into my taxi.") And I learned to love the vibrancy of a crowded market, everyone shouting, while I fought my way along with them to the best products. The next time I visited Portland, I kept wondering where everybody was.

I was also convinced that I had grown unshockable. In our two years in Hong Kong I had survived not only culture shock, but had kept up my spirits through nine cases of food poisoning, two hospitalizations and a fire that burned up everything we owned. (On the bright side, I'd lost 15 pounds and had the unmitigated joy of getting insurance money for my husband's old Santana albums.) Then we moved to Indonesia.

We were posted to Medan, a worn-down remnant of what was once a prosperous rubber plantation town in the middle of the Sumatran jungle.

Well, the jungle was still there. To prepare ourselves better, we had watched "The Year of Living Dangerously." How misleading Hollywood is! I came off the plane expecting to see Mel Gibson. Who I got was Malik, a one-toothed driver from the Consulate who giggled incessantly. Now keen to the signs, my husband grabbed my arm before I could turn around and head back to the tarmac. "I saw that damned movie three times," I hissed at him accusingly, "and there was never any guy like that!"

Determined to put on a brave front once I realized that my exit had been cut off, I forced my face into a rigid smile. I smiled when Malik told us, giggling, that our house wouldn't be ready for two months. I grinned throughout the tour he gave us of the town's "best spots" (highlighting Toko Ben, "where you can buy imported food;" a dilapidated storefront with a dozen boxes of old corn flakes, a few cans of soup, some long-life milk and various indistinguishable boxes, their writing obscured by years of dust.) By the time we were shown the "wet market", so called because the shoppers strode ankle-deep in mud, I had begun giggling like Malik. It didn't fool anyone. When we got to the Consulate, the other married officer glanced at me and said to my husband, "Yeah, that's pretty much the way my wife looked on the first day."

It did get better. By the end, I'd even say that Medan was... not so bad. I learned how to cook from scratch. ("Let's see, this recipe calls for a quarter cup of chicken broth. 'Miriam!' I'd call to my maid, 'Go kill a chicken'." I developed the poise to walk serenely through the curious throng that surrounded me every time I left my house, drawn by my red hair and the chance to call out "Hello, mister!" - the only English words everyone seemed to know. We got close to nature from lizards caught in the computer printer to bats fried on the engine of the car. We saw orang-utans in the wild and climbed into a volcano. The pictures are worth a thousand tears.

Returning to the U.S. after two years in Medan, I came close to a nervous breakdown standing in front of the mile-long cereal aisle at Safeway ("How do I choose?" I wailed. "At Toko Ben, when you wanted cereal, they just handed you a box and you paid.") Arriving at rush hour on the first day of our assignment to Washington, D.C., I stared with foreign eyes at all the women in suits and tennis shoes, then doubled over in stomach cramps. I had to be carried up to our hotel room. So it has gone with every new home.

In truth, I love our globalized lifestyle. Each new post has expanded our perspectives on life, raised our energy levels, refreshed our marriage, allowed us to become new people. Maybe even the culture shock has been a good thing. Perhaps it's the essential first step, opening the eyes like a too-hot swig of black coffee. I guess you could call it shock therapy.

Envelope Thief

Erzsi Deak

It's a long way down to the food section of the Monoprix on rue de Rennes in Paris Sixième.

You try scaling the nearly 90 degree escalator down down down to the bowels of Paris with a 14-month-old lashed into a bulky baby stroller. While the rest of the Sixth *arrondissement* sports high fashion and the Luxembourg Gardens, not-to-forget a few of Paris' legendary literary hotspots such as Brasserie Lipp or Les Deux Magots or Café Le Flore, the Monoprix is supposed to represent no-nonsense shopping for food, clothes, soap, screws, you-name-it except for the thing you really need and saw last week but is long gone, never to be replaced. It's a little bit of a glamorized K-mart, if you will.

You've made it down, the toddler is still with you, after thrilling at the thought of slipping through the belt and making her own way head first, and after the stroller wheels decided they liked independence, too, and went straight into the wall like a first-time driver, nearly catapulting you over the stroller and into the cosmetic counter filled with beautifying possibilities. But then, no one seems to notice you or your near-fatal accident, so on you go to the food, slightly out-of-breath but trying to remain cool as you curse the damn escalator and whoever designed the store with the needs of daily life hidden underground in the back.

The shopping goes well enough. Not much to talk about there; though, I'd avoid the vegetables at this place since they always look tired. At this point the 14-month old thinks it's time to holler and demands a bottle or at least some attention because she is OVER tired. As the other patrons move away from you and your noisy child, you nearly trip over an ornery-looking dog sporting a winter sweater, his extended leash allowing him free roam of the aisle. You remember the French fondness for dogs.

Recovering from the tricky leash and canine, you look non-chalant, scowl like a local at the vegetables, request some ricotta cheese and are given Cantal, all the time thinking as you look at the hard brick, "Jeez, ricotta in the States was always soft and watery." But who knows, maybe you're wrong. You tend to trust THEM more than yourself anymore because you're operating on a different planet, at least that's what it feels like, and the rules must be different here, since nothing ever makes sense. Eventually you'll learn to trust yourself, but for the first few years in your life as an etrangère in this city, you believe they know all and you know nothing. So you take your hard cheese (wondering how you'll stuff the pasta), skip the meat and pick up light-weight stuff like laundry detergent and juice. That's about all that fits in your baby stroller, so you head to the check-out.

Whew. The line is short, everything is going to plan. It's 4:55 p.m. on a gray, wet day in December in Paris. You still have to get to the post office and mail newsy letters and entertaining magazine articles (that you've written) back home.

Better arrange the goods here, since the detergent is trying to escape the non-existent basket beneath the stroller and the juices are about to crash to the floor. We won't talk about the cheese. So you park in what you view as a benign location - near the envelope display. You are proud because you are *out of the way*. The baby's nearly asleep now. Maybe you can sneak in a coffee at Le Flore on boulevard Saint Germain. But what's this, someone is talking to you, or rather, alternating between muttering and yelling at you. "Pardon?" you say, confused by the woman's words and interest in you at all. *"Vendeuse!"* you think she screams. *"Vendeuse d'enveloppes!"* You tell her as politely as possible that you are not the envelope saleswoman and maybe she should direct her calls to someone more appropriately dressed, say someone in one of those sexy Monoprix, white and pink concierge housecoats. You move the stroller over a few inches. She is not amused and is getting louder.

You pretend to ignore her, just as everyone else seems to be doing better than you are.

But she is insistent and is going to wake up the baby, who you wish wouldn't take a nap at 5 p.m., but that's the way it goes, but now that she's asleep, the coffee is sounding great and this woman could ruin that *grand crème* in the sky for you. The woman, who is probably over 60 with garish face paint and a coif bordering on that of Frankenstein's bride, except in a hotter shade of rust, is pointing at you. People are starting to stare now. *"Vendeuse d'enveloppes!"*

She's beginning to bug you. Why doesn't she ask somebody else for help? Can't she see you are a mother with groceries and a need to go to the post office and have a cup of dreamy java? You wish you carried a portable phone or could even find a booth so you could call and bitch to your husband about this damn country. But then you remember he's having a drink with a business buddy and is saying things like, "Oh, yes, the move's gone well, thanks. My wife's making a great adjustment and everybody's happy."

So you lose it. And you lose it in English, because, quite frankly, you don't know how to call her a 'cretin' or a 'peasant' and the F word works so nicely. She ignores you and continues to bellow for an envelope saleswoman. You drive off through the pens and pencils and kids' backpacks for school, past the lipsticks and hair dyes, to the up escalator. She follows. *"Vendeuse d'enveloppes!"* She's pointing her crooked finger at you again and glaring at you like you've stolen her first born.

And then you get it. Then you finally hear what she is saying. But she's still behind you, mounting the moving stairs, trying to catch up: *"Voleuse d'enveloppes! Voleuse d'enveloppes!"* (Envelope thief!)

You make it up to the street level, smile as you pass the guard. She's in conference with him now, jabbing her fist in your direction. Every other word you hear: "... *enveloppes!* ... *voleuse!*" The guard points her to the door.

You contemplate your next move. The post office is right across the street. Better make a dash for it. It's starting to rain again and that coffee is calling your name.

East Meets West

Camilla Lee

My husband and I stood below the cherry trees and argued on a Saturday in March, in the early afternoon. With my back to the wind, I held out the unfolded city map of Tokyo. It flapped a bit, and we tried to pinpoint the location of a restaurant, recommended in a guidebook. According to this book, the restaurant was somewhere near the cemetery in which we stood. My L.L. Bean tote bag rested on the ground. It contained another guidebook, a subway map, and a book of one thousand useful Japanese phrases. We were not tourists, my husband and I, but expatriates. We had been living in Tokyo for six weeks.

"Let's get on with this business of eating. I need food," I said.

My husband said, "I'd rather go home and have a peanut butter sandwich. It's a lot easier, and cheaper."

"That's not the point. We're having this nice Japanese culture day, in case you hadn't noticed." The sarcasm felt good. Besides, I knew if he went home he'd spend the rest of the day watching CNN. All week long he worked hard at trying to grasp the subtleties of his Japanese office. It was up to me to put together our week-end diversions.

This Saturday outing had gone well, so far. We'd visited an old section of the city, where the original township of Edo had been established. The walking tour from the guidebook included two small shrines, an Edo-period calligrapher's supply shop, still in business, and a folk art museum. We skipped the museum, couldn't find the calligraphers', and enjoyed the quiet settings of the two Shinto shrines. We'd walked a lot for one morning. It was way past lunchtime.

Now we stood beneath the cherry trees, arguing the classic arguments which stem from weariness and hunger, and are usually fueled by things quite small. It was not just to do with being lost in this charming, confusing neighborhood that made us irritable. It was the disorientation in our lives. The comforting pattern of the day-to-day had yet to be developed. Ordinary things, like food shopping and eating out, involved a huge amount of effort. I didn't know how to buy rice, and missed Uncle Ben's with the directions on the box. The currency confused me; I was never sure what color bill to pull from my wallet. The numbers seemed enormous. A ten thousand yen note covered one average trip to the grocery store. My "to do" list was long, but errands were slow to complete, and I kept taking naps. Because the doctrine of my Yankee upbringing taught me not to complain, I went about my days, cheerful enough. But standing in that cemetery filled with cherry trees, I began to weaken. I hadn't felt this homesick since I'd gone away to camp in sixth grade.

For lunch the guidebook suggested a noodle restaurant that had been run by a samurai family for several generations. The book had the Japanese characters - three single, lacy, forms of *kanji* - printed beside the phonetic spelling of the restaurant's name. We couldn't find it. In this neighborhood, there were no signs anywhere that we were able to read. Only Japanese characters. Being illiterate gave me a sense of panic. We compared the characters in the guidebook to the ones on the restaurant signs, and could not find an exact match. Yet I was determined to finish this Saturday outing with an interesting Japanese meal. That picture was in my mind. All over Tokyo the cherry trees had blossomed, but the day was windy, and erratic gusts blew petals about. My husband and I stood arguing about where to eat on a ground that looked like pink snow.

The sandwich idea at home was also tempting, but it was cowardly. It took courage to walk into a restaurant while heads turned and conversations stopped. It happened to us all the time, particularly in the remote and more interesting neighborhoods. In my Japanese language lessons I had only, so far, mastered my address. I hadn't advanced to "Eating Out," Chapter Three, with the drawing of the smiling waiter. In fact, I always imagined the staff in restaurants playing stone/paper/

scissors to determine who'd wait on us, the foreigner customers. It was humiliating to be handed a menu you couldn't read. I always ordered *tempura soba*, a standard on all menus, but I was tiring of it, and eager to try something else.

We gave up trying to find that one restaurant, and decided to settle for a substitute. I had imagined a quiet place with tatami mats and waitresses padding silently about in kimono. Leaving the cemetery, we walked in the direction of the subway. Occasionally I'd stop to peer through the curtains of a restaurant, but it always felt threatening. Nothing seemed right. I was angry at my husband for never caring about food, the way I did. I was angry at the Japanese for creating such a confusing city. The streets not only meander, but they have no names, which I thought remarkable. The natives themselves are often lost.

Brooding, I dragged behind my husband through a residential area with little modern houses and laundry hanging in every yard. An old man was pruning one of the many bonsai trees he had along his front stoop. We exchanged hearty *kon-ni-chi-was*, the first word in Chapter One. Soon we got to a busy avenue, and could see in the distance the big complex of Ueno Station, where many train and subway lines connect. We could also see, along the avenue, a line of fast food restaurants.

"McDonald's. Great. Let's go," my husband said.

I stayed sullen. Even in America I never went to McDonald's. I have my standards. But McDonald's in Japan, on a sunny day with scattering cherry blossoms? What a thought. On the other hand there were the Golden Arches, and our blood sugar was low.

As we went through the doors, a young woman in a McDonald's dress and little cap was standing to one side. She said in a complicated phrase, "It is my pleasure to serve you." Then, bending from the waist, she bowed a deep bow. Escorting us to the food counter, she presented, with her white-gloved hand, the shortest line in which to stand. When she felt confident that we'd be all right on our own, she bowed again, and returned to her spot by the door.

The testy mood I'd arrived with was quickly sliding away. Of course I could not read the menu but the beautiful color photographs of Big Macs and French fries were universally understandable. I could communicate.

The restaurant was busy; we ate upstairs. Two older women wearing the housewife kind of cotton kimono - a custom disappearing with the grandmother generation - were eating at the table next to ours. One had on rhinestone-rimmed glasses and they both had dyed black hair the color of shoe polish. Chatting at a fast pace, they finished up their coffee and cardboard-boxed pies. Then, apparently deciding to go back downstairs to get more coffee, they both stood up. First, mid-chatter, they bowed quick little bows to us to apologize for squeezing through our close-together tables. Then they took some coins from their purses, and left the purses, fat with credit cards and yen, on top of their vacated table. This way their table would stay reserved. My husband and I stared at these unattended wallets, left behind in total trust, with awe. It was as though we were admiring a shrine or a cherry tree in bloom. Stealing, to the Japanese, is something that happens only in other countries. In time the ladies returned with their coffee, bowed and clucked again as they slid by, and continued with their conversation.

We ate in silence for a while. Then my husband said, "Maybe after lunch we could go find that folk art museum." Happy with this suggestion, I nodded, and finished the last of my Coke. Pulling the map from my bag, I unfolded it across the table. We pinpointed the train station, this McDonald's, and the short walk to the museum. I also pinpointed a specific sensation ripple through me. At that moment I started my friendship with Japan.

Things We're Made Of

Patricia S. Roberts

Ten years ago I said *I do* and because *I really did*, I forfeited my name, shed my job, lost my income, gave up my apartment and, as if smoking a final cigarette before execution, I relished one last American donut before flying off with my new husband to a land quite foreign and very far away. As soon as the donut was gone I realized so too was I: Gone.

"Something's missing," I announced to the guy who would now carry my luggage for the rest of my life. "*Me.*" As our departure date loomed, the girl I knew grew harder to see. Even the debts I had nurtured for years disappeared.

"Not to worry, you're Mrs. New Name now," my husband answered reassuringly.

"Not enough," I pleaded. Since my bio sheet had been red-lined and rewritten overnight, I explained that I needed something to validate my existence, something that hinted at the person I was: a person who ate refried beans cold from the can, walked under ladders by choice, chose bowls over bumps. Then it dawned on me, it wasn't *something* I needed, it was *some things*.

I wasn't going anywhere without my *stuff*.

"You want to haul that garage sale with us?" my husband asked incredulously. "That junk is an indictment of the Human Condition! We agreed it would stay in storage." In the end he proved to be a good listener so, as we touched down into the gray swirl of smog over Istanbul, I was comforted by the thought that as I followed my new husband into a new life, 20 boxes filled with proof of my past lives followed closely behind.

We set up house in an old wooden *yali** on the shore of the Bosphorus Straits. For one week I unpacked, tearing first into wedding gifts and saving the best for last: my boxes of long-for-

---

* Yali is an old, wooden Turkish villa.

gotten junk. I broke into each carton slowly, the ripping tape sending a painful echo through the empty house.

When the boxes were unpacked, I was left surrounded by a yard-sale temple to my former self: 12 stacks of magazines (old); Tea Room depression glass (pink); letters (love); beveled mirror (bought at Doris Rutherford's tag sale when I was 14); authentic Squirmy Rooter (bachelorette party favor); red tulle dress from Screaming Mimi's in New York (good old days); topiary trees; painting called Summerstorm; birdhouse; hooked rabbit rug; windchimes; Weber grill; baskets; wooden American Flag; holiday survival kit (candy corn, whirlygig Santa, garlands of stars, sparklers).

We hung up the windchimes, stuck the birdhouse in a tree, put the American flag on the kitchen wall and all summer grilled greasy fish on the Weber. To my husband's dismay, I hung Summerstorm in the livingroom. It was a huge pea green oil, painted by a heartbreaker posing as an artist in Boulder, Colorado. Days later our new housecleaner, Mestana, doused it with Pledge, upgrading it on the meteorological chart from storm to hurricane. She had never seen an aerosol can. They didn't have such things in the *gecekondos*, the shanty towns around the city. I suspected she was part gypsy as she loved to dance and take down her hair as soon as she crossed my threshold, while other maids kept theirs hidden under drab scarves. One day she sat on the floor, cried, and explained how good her husband was to her: he beat her only once a day, she said.

By autumn we were used to the muezzin's round-the-clock call to prayer and each day rose blinking into Doris Rutherford's mirror, wiping our eyes clean of the black Istanbul coal dust which settled to earth each night. From our terrace we watched the maritime world challenge the fierce current and were especially entertained by Soviet freighters which played cat and mouse with the pesky CIA boat as they cut a wake from the Black Sea south to the Mediterranean. On foggy days we peered suspiciously into the water as it often happened that boats went off course in the whiteout and slammed into the banks, wiping out dining rooms in the process.

As if throwing out seed to attract birds, we opened the candy corn and threw a Halloween Party. Ninety-three people came, including a guest draped head-to-toe in a black cloak. I complimented him on his well-conceived nun's costume, earning a lecture on the laws of Islam and how they apply to women. I won't forget the word *chador* and on gray days (and there were many that got snagged on the minarets straddling East and West) I often wished for my own *chador*, a simple piece of black cloth to hide everything from laugh lines to panty lines. But *chadors* were not a religious fashion in Turkey so instead I dragged out years of magazines from my collection and hid within the pages until it was safe to come out, reading the same articles over and over "Mastering Eggplant," "How To Keep the Fun in Marriage."

I was alone, but not. My mother's voice spoke from the topiary trees that gave life to our rented table *("Tell stories with your things, darling. For Christmas cover your topiaries with holly... hang baskets in the kitchen, fill them with sage...")* and my father winked back from the light reflecting from my glass collection which he started for me. I remember our first find, in a Greenwich Village antique shop. We came across a vase in mint condition and my father wore down the salesman until he reached his price. I spent the following years drinking linden tea in Istanbul's Grand Bazaar practicing, over and over, his art of negotiation.

A year went by. Then two. The only thing that seemed to grow were the piles of magazines, which became the topic of discussion between my husband and me during late night dinners. Leaning towers of dog-eared issues flanked our bed and crowded tables. When seasons of beauty treatments and recipes started overflowing from our spare room I began filing away the articles I couldn't live without: "Infertility: Could it be you?" "Thinner Thighs Through Thalasso" and "Ten Tips for Emotional Health."

"You're AWOL in those pages!" my husband claimed one day, threatening to throw everything in the Bosphorus.

"Knowledge is such a burden! I can't dismiss it all - these are my connection to the world!" I said, before huffing off, threatening to renew my subscriptions. When he fell asleep, I pulled out my box of letters (love) and read each word written by Carmine, which was not my husband's name. Until morning I flipped madly through old *House & Gardens*, vintage *Vogues*, *Redbooks*. My fingers tired as fast as my eyes and I suddenly found that so many words of advice weighed heavily. I ached for what I thought was "home" but soon discovered I was really looking for the two-dimensional promises on each page. Maybe home was where I was. I began throwing magazines away.

As our third Turkish winter dissipated, we painted the living room (I had given Summerstorm to Mestana and was left with a huge white square on the wall). When that was done I moved on to the spare bedroom with a can of buttercup paint. The room was empty, but it wouldn't be for long. I was now reading for two.

When I finished the yellow trim, my husband came in, carrying one of my old boxes. He rummaged around and pulled out the pink and blue hooked rabbit rug I hadn't seen in years. Without a word he placed it in the center of the room and we listened as it chased the echoes away.

Acclimatization Hah

Christa Weil

As an American abroad, I've grown accustomed to the shades of gray involved in acclimating to foreign countries. Paris was my first adopted home; two years later I moved to London. Today, after considerable exposure to the elements of these cities, I've come to a conclusion, and one umbrella statement serves to say it all. The weather is not to my liking.

The weather was not always to my liking in New Haven, Princeton, or New York City either, but there I had grown inured. Here adaptation is virtually impossible, because the weather patterns don't stay put long enough. To my mind, the half-hourly fluctuations and meteorological whimsy of the northwestern edge of the European Union is evidence of instability on a continental scale. I trust many fellow expatriates would agree that the issue is more common and current than the 'Euro', and staggering as any mad cow. As an impartial American, let me state frankly: vast parcels of the European continent are climatically challenged. The technocrats in the community must precipitate solutions, no matter how loudly nationalist Britons may beef. Unite and share the wealth with the partners to the south. Throw those borders open, and I mean all the way. Let the sun shine in.

Naturally, my friends back in France would have an opinion: to wit, this is all imbecile. But of course they would. The ability to walk bareheaded and nonplussed through drenching rain is one of the lesser-known Gallic strengths, stemming from a sublime disregard for life's minor afflictions. In Paris, a sudden squall garners much the same response as an underdressed tourist: ignore it, it will go away. The attitude toward unpleasant weather finds its ultimate expression in the stone gargoyles that crown the cathedrals. Back home, rain gutters are ugly conduits that people don't like to think about, especially come leaf season in autumn. In Paris, rain gutters are ugly conduits that people pay hard cash to see, and have rolls of pictures to prove it.

On the Boulevard St. Germain, there is a clothing store unlike any other on that elegant street. Its name is *Vêtements pour Pays Chauds*. Clothes for Warm Countries. The store exists, I imagine, because the farther-flung regions of the Francophone purview lack a comprehensive selection of sea-island cotton, tropical-weight worsted, and fashionable pith helmets. Fair enough. But what does the name tell you about the local climate?

The British have a different take on their meteorological condition. Unlike the French, they do carry umbrellas, and acknowledge their "beastly weather" with apologetic half-smiles. But those smiles tell a tale. In the summer of 1995, the city experienced an unprecedented sequence of flawless skies. What was all the guff about bad English weather, I wondered, having just moved to the country. Meanwhile, natives were eyeing the forecasts with increasing desperation. Finally, one northern-born shopkeeper broke down and admitted, "I canna' stan' a skay withoot cloods," he said. "I canna' think straight withoot cloods." A few months later, when normal weather was back, I understood what he meant. I feel the same way aboot blue.

Recently, I went native and bought a Barbour jacket. These coats famously keep out rain and wind because they are thoroughly impregnated with lanolin, the greasy stuff that waterproofs sheep. The coat does have a remarkable repellent effect; when I pulled it out of its bag to show my husband, the smell was so rank I had to shove it back in, fearing serious damage to our sniffers. I called the Barbour clerk and pleaded for a solution. Over the roar of the ventilation equipment, he shouted, "Hang it, madam. Outdoors, in the wind. It is the only effective way to get rid of the... the state of affairs." And so, for the past week, my new coat has been bared to the elements: flapping in the wind, dripping in the rain, impassively taking in the night air. I brought it back indoors yesterday, and guess what. It still smells. And now it's infested with spiders. But I do understand more about sheep, why they're so placid.

If they can put up with this day in and day out, the poor dears can put up with anything.

Did you know that Eskimos have forty words for snow? Of course you did, you're sick of hearing about it already. But, forty is a drop in the bucket compared to the BBC's synonyms for rain. "Drip, drizzle, splash, sprinkle, another spot of wet, I'm afraid." Zap! The satellite spins to the French weather goddesses of TF1 and M6. With forecasters this *magnifique*, who cares about the coming deluge? And why indeed spoil the lines of that jacket by wearing a blouse underneath, especially with such a fine tan... Zap! Flip Spiceland. I say it again, because I like to. Flip Spiceland. A name that promises sunny skies ahead, even when CNN weathermaps don't, a name like a skiff that's Molucca-bound, our very own port in the storm. Flip always makes it seem fresh when reporting the "possibility of rain" in northern Europe, or, for that matter, "dry conditions" in northern Africa. That, and the snazzy black suit, is why he gets my vote as the satellite age's Weather God.

My fellow Americans, accustomed to beautiful and spacious skies, don't seem to share my little obsession when they come to Europe; indeed they seem to have preoccupations of their own. Consider the typical first-timers to Paris. There they sit in a charming café, recharging after visits to Notre-Dame and Sainte-Chapelle. Having taken in these breathtaking embodiments of man's highest aspirations, one topic inevitably dominates conversation: "Wonder what it's doing right now in Cincinnati?" They needn't bother checking the back page of "USA Today." The weather is always much better back home.

Until you're actually back there, of course. Then the clouds tumbling down from Sacré-Cœur are sanctified in memory as nothing short of majestic, and England was so very green... but I'm getting ahead of myself, and I'd best get up and shut the windows. You know why. It's getting gloomy. You can bet your brolly that, pretty soon, it's gonna pour.

Me Versus the Dust

Gisela Pacho

My most vivid memory of Africa is of being filthy, coated in orange dust from the roots of my hair to the spaces between my toes. My clothes developed a hopeless and permanent orange tinge. I gave up on wearing light colors after about one week in Uganda, but fought the dust until I could fight no more.

I accompanied my husband on *his* dream job. But I, jobless, hot, and without a working telephone to call a friend, needed a focal point for my anger. I found my enemy and it was none of the obvious choices. It was *dust*. The very African earth itself.

My first orange dirt battles were fought in the sink of our Kampala Sheraton hotel room, scrubbing out a 3-inch diagonal orange stain from the front of a white blouse, purchased specially for our African adventure. The stain had come from the seatbelt of our Suzuki jeep.

I made a game out of determining how long certain expatriates had been in Uganda by the look of their clothes. The tennis players with deep orange rings embedded around the ankles of their socks were obvious.

When we finally moved into a house and got some pets, our dogs were even a shade of orange, and we thought it was their natural color until we washed them. They emerged from the bath a shiny golden brown and proceeded immediately to roll around in the dirt as if we'd stripped them naked of their identities.

Our house came with a washing machine in the form of a small cleaning woman named Mary. The first time Mary washed our clothes I felt awkward at the thought of having her work so hard and sweat just so I could have clean tennis socks. I was ashamed at having a servant. But as I saw the results my shame dissipated. For weeks Mary scrubbed our clothes senseless, and she didn't seem to mind. The clothes were frayed, but they had no trace of dust. My white socks were white, and everything smelled good.

The orange dust defeated, I rejoiced until the day that an electric washer arrived in a shipment from the States. To my surprise, Mary nearly broke out in song. She had never seen a washing machine but she knew what one was. No more hand washing.

I was skeptical. This scrawny American washer could be no match for Mary, and I was right. It would surrender to the orange dust.

For six months Mary conducted what amounted to experiments in tinting clothes, washing reds and whites together in hot water, and so on. My shirts became a swirl of irreparable rainbows and Mary apologized. Mary would pull the ruined wet bundles out of the washing machine and say "Sorry, Madam, it is spoiled." Was this my punishment for preferring Mary to the washing machine?

Not only were the colors running, but my enemy the dust was winning. No bleach, no detergent, no machine could match Mary's scrubbing action. The days of white whites were gone. Mary even began hauling her own clothes from her home four miles away to use our washing machine. Mary was determined never to wash a stitch of clothes, hers or anyone else's, by hand again.

Over time I came to accept my faded dusty garments. The dust was becoming part of my identity, just like my dogs. I was a seasoned expat who hadn't had a home leave in ages, and I wore it with a vengeance.

Moldy Blues
in the Philippines

Isabel Huggan

Arriving for the first time in the Philippines and stepping out of the Ninoy Aquino International Airport into the Manila night, I expected the air to be cool because it was dark. Mark that up as my first mistake.

It was like walking smack into a warm washcloth. Until I got into a waiting van and was shaken free by a frigid blast from the air conditioner, I felt glued to myself like a licked envelope...even a little panicky, as I gasped for breath, trying to inhale air with the texture of thick, soft cotton.

Goodness me, heat and humidity. How Canadian to start with the weather instead of speaking about the Rich Cultural Opportunities. How typical, how boring.

Well maybe so, but until you adjust to the climate when you move from one country to another, you just can't think abut anything else: it is Numero Uno on the Adaptation List. The high temperatures of Southeast Asia (in the 30's Centigrade) can definitely be a shock to your personal thermostat, but worse, everything seems damp to the touch - your skin, your clothes, your bed sheets, your towels even *before* you attempt to dry yourself after the showers you take every few hours in an attempt to feel human again. Even the slightest movement makes you perspire - oh, why be fancy? Sweat like a pig.

"It ain't the heat, it's the humidity." NEVER has that hoary old chestnut been more true - and if the chestnut's in Manila it'll be fuzzy with mold. Honestly, you've got to keep moving - stand still, and you get athlete's foot.

You think I'm kidding? In the rainy season there are half-page ads in the newspapers for Tinactin to combat "body fungus" - fighting jungle rot is a way of life in this part of the world. I had always thought "Man against Nature" meant doing battle with a snowshovel but that just goes to show how culturally narrow my life has been.

You suddenly find yourself susceptible to a multitude of grungy, yeasty skin diseases (women with large breasts - you know, the ones that fold over - are particularly at risk). You discover that the true function of your body is to act as a breeding ground for bacteria. You learn that your fine leather shoes will turn an odd shade of green if you leave them untended, and that your Nikes will sprout toadstools unless you keep them in a well-lit closet. In our house we have a small walk-in "hot room" where two 100-watt bulbs burn night and day so that our suitcases, hiking boots, winter clothes and video tapes don't succumb to tropical decay....

Eventually you pick up these coping tactics, but that's not to say it's easy or quick - the operative word is "eventually." You are in the First Stage of Culture Shock, honey, whether you want to be or not. It may last days, weeks, or months, but until you settle down to the drastic truth - this weather is the pits but there's no way to change it - you're gonna keep fighting a force stronger than you are.

You learn not to leave food out on the kitchen counters but it may take a few nasty encounters with marching ants to condition you properly. Butter left out of the fridge melts and turns rancid so you get used to bread with little hard chunks on it, or even better you learn to eat without butter, *comme les français*. Soon, as if you've always done it, you'll keep sugar, flour, pasta and cereal in the freezer. In no time your cat, like ours, will only deign to eat dry catfood if it's still ice-cold and crunchy...

You get used to having geckos (small, nearly translucent lizards) living in your house as welcome guests because they eat insects, but nevertheless they'll still startle you witless as they dash up walls or scamper out of the bathroom sink. You may even have a tuko or two indoors, although your house staff will express great fear of these larger, speckled lizards, not because of their loud evening calls (Tuuuuu-ko!) but because folktales have it that if ever they land on you, their sucker-feet cannot be removed from skin without much bloodshed. (Not true, but nevertheless, the maid may call in the gardener with his machete to dispense with your family tuko unless you intervene.) You can live with God's creatures in harmony - you simply learn not to turn on the CD player without first checking if one of them has left droppings in the machine, or worse, is still sleeping there. Yikes! Mozart à la gecko!

The lizards are charming compared to that other permanent resident, the thumb-sized and ubiquitous cockroach. You can try any number of methods involving sprays, traps and powders, but you will simply, in the end, get used to that awful scurry when you enter a dark room and turn on the light.

You eventually acknowledge a heartless cruelty you never knew you possessed, as you sit and watch with cheerful satisfaction a RAID-sprayed cockroach breathing its last with its little bug legs waving in the air. The thing is, there are more where that one came from. This place is teeming with life.

In a few weeks or so you've got the hang of it, and if you weren't a neatness freak before you arrived, you are now, buying yet another container of lemon-scented rubbing alcohol with which you wipe everything from kitchen counters to your own skin. And you discover that your anti-fungal and insect dealings are as child's play compared to the more delicate social and cultural adjustments you need to make.

Some North Americans are initially fooled into thinking that integration will be a piece of cake because the Philippines seems "so much like home." Because of the political and cultural influence of the United States, Filipinos have indeed adopted language, clothing, customs and foods which are American in origin and nature. Never fear, a McDonald's is always near.

But the differences, although not immediately apparent, exist. Making your way into real friendships - or even workable work-day relationships - will exact a great deal of emotional toil, and good honest sweat. If you are here long enough, and care enough, you'll do it... You do get used to the climate, and you do make friends.

And you may even, after a few years, find yourself doing as I have done these past few months (now into my fourth year), complaining about the cold, and getting up in the night for a light blanket.

Wetter But Wiser

Ellen Newmark

I used to live in Germany. Once, in a trip home to California, I found myself in a supermarket watching gratefully as a young man packed my groceries into a plastic bag. My emotions surged. What a country!

Swept by a wave of patriotism, I tipped him five bucks. He gaped in surprise, but only because he didn't understand. He hadn't been with me that rainy morning in Germany when I went out to phone a plumber.

Due to the local practice of waiting five weeks for a phone, I had to brave the chilly wet weather if my sink was ever to work again. I grabbed my old black umbrella and stepped out; it was only a light rain.

The plumber didn't answer and almost no one in Germany uses answering machines. Disappointed and already damp, I decided to walk a few more blocks to buy a tiny bit of consolation in the village bakery.

A German bakery could weaken the most stoic dieter, but, determined to show restraint, I pointed primly to the croissants. Then I saw the cream puffs. Seductive, downright erotic.

Immediately, I succumbed to the Mad Sugar Lust well known in German bakeries. My index finger assumed a life of its own: cream puffs, apple strudel, fruit tarts, Black Forest Torte... When I came to my senses, there was a line of little paper packages on the counter about a yard long. I waited for the *Fräulein* to bag it all up for me, but she was already waiting on the next customer - a German woman carrying a cute wicker basket into which she neatly packed rye bread and strudel.

Aha! The Basket. A common local practice.

Resigned to go bagless, I scooped up the goodies, arranging them so that the fruit tarts didn't crush the cream puffs and balancing the delicate Torte on top. With everything cradled precariously, I raised my umbrella and stepped out into the rain, which had become a little heavier.

I got almost halfway home before I sneezed. Of course, the Black Forest torte plopped onto the pavement, but, fortunately, the rain was so hard by then that the whipped cream and cherries washed away very quickly.

An elderly lady stopped to watch it dissolve. Then she looked at me with, well, Teutonic disgust. That's when I realized that my nose was running. I tried to get a tissue out of my purse without putting down the umbrella. No good. The tarts fell off, and when I lunged to save them, the apple strudel slipped out sideways. After I accidentally stepped in the tarts, I noticed how much easier that made it for the rain to wash them away. So I stepped on the strudel too.

Then the umbrella broke. The paper around the top cream puff quickly soaked through and dribbled a smear of goo down the front of my coat. I shoved a soggy croissant into each pocket, clasped the last cream puff to my breast and sprinted, nose and hair dripping, through a torrential downpour.

As I stood panting inside my front door, I discovered that the croissants were smashed flat and embedded with wet paper. I threw them away. The cream puff was damaged too, but I ate that sucker standing up.

Five bucks for a bagger? If the bag is plastic, you bet.

Ancient Arts
and Modern
Misunderstandings

Leza Lowitz

I've often been mystified by certain occurrences here in Tokyo that have seemed baffling at best or inefficient at worst. Were they strategies or slip-ups? It's often hard to know. Take the time I got a $250.00 parking ticket, which came in the form of an orange plastic box locked to the mirror that only the police can unlock. Rather than suffer the ignominy of this day-glow pox upon one's automobile, one must drive the car to the nearest policebox to have it unlocked. After, and only after one has paid the ticket, of course.

I drove to the nearest policebox and tried to pay. When I showed my International Driver's License, the rookie cop exclaimed, "California? Oh, Miami Vice," drawing an imaginary gun from an imaginary holster in a move that was far more John Wayne than Don Johnson. My place of birth settled, he began to fill out the forms and suddenly stopped cold. Japanese licenses had one less numerical digit, so there were not enough boxes on the form. One too many X's for the box.

Horrors for the rookie bureaucrat.

To be fair, there's a reason things are so tightly controlled in Japan, particularly in the big cities. The places are so packed with people in such small spaces that there's very little margin for error. The city, surprisingly, works. However, when confronted with the unexpected, all hell breaks loose.

The head cop was apologetically summoned. He looked at the form, looked at the license, looked at me, scratched his head, and left the room. Headquarters was called. I was handed the phone and after being transferred to untold recesses of some concrete building somewhere, I was connected to an English-speaking officer who explained that my license had one digit more than the Japanese licenses, and that appropriate actions were being taken to find an appropriate form for my inappropriate license. A form with an extra box for my X.

I'd just read *The Japanese Art of War: Understanding the Culture of Strategy* and was curious: Was what I saw as total incompetence and inefficiency really the ancient "art of the advantage" used by samurai of old? And hadn't I used it myself to throw these opponents into disarray? I doubted it, but you never knew.

In order to understand modern Japanese psychology and behavior, the theory went, you had to consider the influence of centuries of military rule. Perhaps people were still so imbued with martial traditions that what appeared like mystery was probably method. I doubted that, too, but this was a perfect observation ground.

After our negotiations had continued unsuccessfully for several hours and midnight had come and gone, two drunk businessmen came in to vomit in the rest room. I enlisted them to broker my release. They were my only hope, and it didn't matter what they said. They were witnesses whose presence offered a way to take the heat off the cops. That much I understood. If the cops let me go, it would then be because of these strangers, so they wouldn't be held responsible. The drunk businessman suggested I apologize. I did. (A sly charade - I'd apologized six times already.)

Now the rookie miraculously produced an "apology form" from the drawer of the desk where he'd been sitting our whole time together. All I had to do was sign at the X and promise I'd never do anything illegal while in Japan. Since this voided the $250.00 fee, I signed.

Some advice from the brilliant Japanese warriors of old included, "Sneak across the ocean in broad daylight," "Plunge into a fire to pull off a robbery," "Borrow a corpse to bring back a spirit," and, finally, "it is best to run."

And that is just what I was about to do.

But where to park? I asked the rookie cop, who asked the chief cop, since rookies aren't supposed to have answers, and certainly not answers to anything important.

"Up the street." The boss pointed to the very area I had been tagged.

"Yes, but isn't that place illegal?" I knew full well it was. The sign said so, clearly, and I'd just been through an ordeal because of it.

"If you move your car before 8 a.m. you should be okay."

I thanked him and left the police box with a gentle bow. So much for forms and strategies. I'd take ancient arts and modern misunderstandings over them any day.

American Trash

Tara McKelvey

"What are the biggest differences between Europeans and Americans?" I asked Wlodek Zagorski, a Polish biologist who has spent time in the U.S. and France.

Europeans gravitate toward urban centers, "ideally to an apartment right on the Champ Elysees," he says. Americans dream of moving to the suburbs. Europeans are formal at mealtimes. When you fly from one European city to another, for example, there is a ritual for serving tea. An airline hostess extends a plastic tray toward you, and you place your cup on top. Then she fills the cup and offers you milk and sugar. In the friendly skies above America, you just wave the tea cup in her direction. Then she pours you a cup. On a grander scale, the basic point of departure for Europeans is negative, while Americans start everything in a positive way.

Personally, I'm convinced the biggest difference between Europeans and Americans is not our urban landscape, our mealtime manners, or our attitudes towards life. It's the way we feel about packaging. Europeans are still living in the Dark Ages when it comes to packaging, and I think I know why. To their credit, Europeans aren't that interested in disposable containers.

On my last trip to New York, I bought a clip-on container designed to carry a disposable coffee cup. This device attaches to the handle of a baby carriage. Now I can bring along a cup of coffee when I take my baby for a walk. I proudly showed off this contraption to my Polish babysitter, and she shook her head and sighed. "Americans!" she said. There's no such thing as take-out coffee in Warsaw, except at an American fast-food joint. When you buy orange juice in Europe, it comes in clunky, cardboard boxes that defy even the thirstiest American.

Noses may crumble off statues in Cracow because of damage done to the environment, but in one respect, Europeans, and especially Poles, are environmentally conscious. Like all Europeans, Poles hate waste. They're more likely to mend a pair of socks than buy a new pair, repair the splintered leg of a chair instead of throwing the whole thing out, and store a used pickle jar for some unknown, future use. Poles recycle. And unlike Americans, they don't need state laws to make them comply.

No wonder my cavalier approach to household goods drives my husband crazy. As a Polish-American, he sides with Europeans when it comes to recycling. He doesn't like the way I throw away Le Clerk shopping bags* instead of washing them out and hanging them on the line to dry. He disapproves of the way I use paper towels instead of cloth ones. Since we moved to Poland, tension between us has continued to mount over this issue. For my husband, the last straw was the November morning when he found a cardboard egg carton in the trash.

He lifted it out of the trash can and looked at it. I'd thrown away the leftover portions of the last night's dinner on top of the egg carton. The egg carton was soaked in spaghetti sauce, and the cardboard was starting to dissolve. "People save these here," he said, shaking his head sadly. I knew he was disappointed in me.

That's when he took a hard line and started a campaign to help mend my wasteful, American ways. First, he suggested I line the kitchen trash can with newspaper instead of using plastic trash bags. I didn't like carrying a sloppy bucket out to the front sidewalk, dumping its contents into the trash and bringing it back to the kitchen. It was a messy process, and I had to clean out the bucket regularly. But I tried to follow his lead.

Then he placed a unilateral ban on milk cartons. "They're expensive," he says. I'm supposed to buy plastic bags of milk, which cost about five cents less.

---

* A Le Clerk shopping bag is a flimsy, almost see-through, common grocery store shopping bag given free and generously to all Le Clerk Shoppers.

"As if the cartons aren't bad enough!" I said.

I still haven't figured out the European carton, even after years of use. A few weeks ago, I walked into the living room with two glasses and a carton of orange juice for an American friend and her Polish husband. I naturally brought along a pair of scissors, since that's the only way I've managed to open the box. My friend's husband looked at me disgustedly. He lifted up the carton and tore it open with his bare hands. But my American friend understood. It is a feat none of us expats, used to fancy packaging, have mastered.

Now my husband wants me to buy the more advanced milk sack. You're supposed to snip off a corner with scissors and then pour the milk into another container. But every time I open a milk sack, I get soaked. I don't like carrying them, either. They bounce along and gurgle in my shopping bag. I feel like I'm carrying home a cow's udder.

I want to protect the environment, run a household and make my husband happy. Especially after I came home the other day and saw the trash heaped on the sidewalk in front of our house. There were juice cartons, boxes of Italian tomato paste and shampoo bottles on the ground. Our Polish-made trash can - a tall, thin metal cylinder - isn't big enough to hold all the things we throw away. I felt ashamed, and I promised myself I would start by cutting down on paper goods.

But then I thought...' Maybe I could bring back a Rubbermaid trash can from the States, the kind that conceals all the trash so you don't even know it's there.' What would I do with the old one? I figured I could just throw it away.

Cheek-to-Cheek

Marion Schmitz-Reiners

Long before it became the fashion in Germany to greet both friends and enemies with a kiss on the cheek, I moved to Belgium. So, when I arrived here, I was relatively unpracticed in this form of interpersonal communication.

Today, over ten years later, I more or less know my way around the Belgian 'kissing jungle.' But the road here has been a rocky one, paved with painful moments and a series of mishaps.

I owe my first social kissing experiences to the relatives of my husband-to-be. They opened their arms wide, pulled me close, and gave me three hearty kisses on the cheeks, left-right-left. I thought this was great. And that's where the misunderstandings started.

Because, in my innocence, I assumed this was the way you did things in Belgium and was happy to oblige. As a socially sensitive person, I used every opportunity I could from then on to give my three kisses on the cheeks. But some of the recipients only wanted to be kissed twice. And others only once. And this of course led to seconds-long silent duels between someone who thought the kissing ritual was over and someone who thought it had only just begun...

After I had endured this situation for a while, I asked a Belgian friend and confidante what the contemporary Belgian state-of-the-art in kissing was really like. She explained things to me carefully. Kissing three times is out - and has been for a long time. If at all, it is used by the peasantry, or in situations where one wants to signify a special, even exclusive, degree of warmth. These days, she told me, the average everyday greeting means kissing only once - no, not even kissing, just breathing. The fleeting indication of a kiss, the brushing of cheeks, is both chic and the surest evidence that you have your proper place in society.

Good enough. I'm a fast learner, so I made the change. But this was the start of another series of misunderstandings.

Because I was now the one who kissed only once! So what was I supposed to do if, after the self-conscious brushing of cheeks, my opposite number offered the other cheek? This called for lightning reflexes. And then yet another cheek? Indeed I was putting people in exactly the situation I had been in for all too long: they wanted to kiss three times, but I only wanted to kiss once. The situation in reverse.

But it's even more complicated than that. You can divide the Belgian social kiss into a number of families or genuses. There is the party kiss, the birthday kiss, the Xmas kiss, the mother-in-law kiss, and the kiss you exchange during a casual encounter in the street, when shopping or in front of the school gates.

All of these genuses can, in turn, be subdivided into species. Kisses are fleeting in the morning, generous in the evening. You just brush cheeks in the summer, but heartily press your lips against the other party's cheek in the winter. It is even possible to differentiate between party kisses, when it's a matter of split seconds and millimeters.

The cool party kiss - normally a single one, ideally with your hands in your jacket pockets, well clear of interfering champagne glasses and cigarettes - can tell volumes. If you feel obliged to kiss someone you don't like, then you simply send a half-breath in the direction of his or her ear. If you're genuinely pleased to see someone again - the sort of thing that can happen at parties - then you plant a kiss more or less in the middle of his or her cheek. If you're secretly in love, but not anxious to show it, then you kiss him or her close to the corner of the mouth. If your kiss happens to land on his or her mouth, then spectators are entitled to think what they want to.

This little game has its charm, after all. As much for those involved as for the onlookers.

But after I'd learned the ropes and rarely got it wrong any longer, I happened to go back to Germany on a visit. And that's where I got into deep trouble.

I saw one of my old acquaintances, someone I didn't particularly like. So I settled for a cool handshake. And what did she do? She embraced me, held me to her bosom for at least half a minute and, what's more, kissed me somewhere on the neck. It seems the kiss on the cheek is out of fashion again in Germany! Women approaching middle age greet one another with a warm embrace. Even men are known to kiss one another. So, once again, I find myself confronted with a ritual dilemma.

What would happen to me in France or Spain? When, oh when, I ask myself despairingly, will someone write an international 'how to' book on kissing?

Inconvenience Store

Jan Kilner

My recollections of Foreign Service assignments are flavored by, and indeed center around, food - shopping for essentials, preparing local specialties and American favorites with available ingredients and, of course, sampling the country's cuisine. The pictures may be hung and the rugs laid down, but I cannot feel settled in a new home until I've figured out where to buy pine nuts and basil, how to get the local butcher to understand what I want and, especially, how to procure and prepare food as the natives do. Of course we have been lucky to have had assignments in France and Turkey, centers of two of the world's *hautes cuisines*. But I realize that even my two years spent in East Berlin - hardly a gastronomic capital - were spiced by food, in this case, cross-cultural misunderstandings at the hunting and gathering stage.

East Berlin was our second assignment, from 1983 to 1985 when the hard-line Communist regime was still going strong. We had been quite successful (we'd thought) in our first posting to Istanbul, making local friends and penetrating the culture (well, we'd learned how to raise our raki glasses and order meze) on a skeleton knowledge of Turkish, often assured by our friends that our command of the language would qualify us for election to the Turkish equivalent of the Academie Française. So I was certain that my college training in German and my good will toward the poor East Germans, oppressed by the Russians, would be my entrée to the society. There were obstacles, like the member of the not-so-secret police who stood guard in front of our apartment. But if the locals couldn't come to us, I could go to them! I would make it a point to avoid the West and live like a native, always using public transportation and shopping locally.

We were lucky enough to have, half a block away, a spanking new "supermarket" (state-owned and run, naturally) called the Kaufhalle. At the first opportunity I marched over to check it out. It was about the size of a 7-Eleven convenience store. I hadn't planned to buy anything yet, just cruise the aisles.

First I passed the "fruit and vegetable section" with its cabbages and turnips and potatoes; the only fruits I saw were on the colorful sign. Later I admired bottled gray peas and such delectable imports as tinned fish from Bulgaria. (The famous East German white asparagus, I was to discover, could only be found in the hard currency stores.) Finally I reached the beer display and realized we could use some. After all, even communist beer had to be good if it was German. Using my keen observational skills, I noticed the other customers turning each bottle over, so I too picked up a bottle and turned it over (I thump watermelons, too, although I'm not sure what I'm listening for). I soon discovered that most of the bottles contained sediment, but I finally chose two which were relatively clear and proceeded to the check-out stand.

When I arrived at the cashier, she rolled her eyes and said something unintelligible about my shopping cart. But I didn't have a shopping cart, and it seemed *that* was the problem. I learned that the check-out technique was for the cashier to take items out of the current customer's basket, ring them up, and place them in the previous customer's basket. After payment, the customer wheeled that cart to a table for loading into personal shopping bags or carts, as his empty basket was left waiting for the next customer. *Alles in Ordnung* (everything is in order), only I, with no cart, had fouled up the system. I slunk out of the store with my beer, vowing to do better next time.

I am a confirmed "reducer, re-user and recycler" of packaging materials so I admired the bottle return system I'd noticed at the Kaufhalle entrance. Having consumed, and perhaps been reinforced by the beer, I returned to the store with my empty bottles. I grabbed a shopping cart, quick learner that I am, and proceeded to the recycling line. The attendant was absent, but everyone was waiting patiently, so I waited too. After he returned, the line didn't move much faster and, being in a hurry, I decided, "What the heck! These bottles, full, cost only twenty-five cents!" Stepping out of line, I placed the bottles in an empty rack and turned to go. Gasps, mumblings and "tsks" came from the line. The attendant actually stood up and yelled, "You can't do that! Which were your bottles?" I pointed meekly to the two lone bottles and he, with a flourish, picked them up, placed them in their proper spot and slammed my deposit into my hand. Devastated, I slunk out of the store once again, this time without purchases.

Not to be daunted, however, I ventured back in a few days, equipped with my empty shopping bag. This time I was going to shop for food. I took a cart, tossed in the empty bag, and proceeded up and down the aisles choosing eggs, milk (it was packaged in plastic bags, but everyone else was buying it), salami, flour, and more beer. I felt pleased with myself until a store employee came up and berated me for having placed my shopping bag in the cart. "How will we know you're not stealing?" she demanded. I started to respond but, met with a cold stare, sheepishly slid the bag over my shoulder - a much more convenient location, I thought, had I wanted to slip in some canned goods. This time I made it through the check-out line and home relatively unscathed. I decided to start leaving our empty bottles outside our door, arguing to myself that the *Hausmeister* could certainly use the extra change.

Encouraged by my successful shopping, and bag over shoulder, I visited the supermarket two days later. I nearly filled my cart (not an easy feat considering the offerings) and was about to go pay, when I realized I'd forgotten eggs. I parked my basket in the last aisle and quickly walked two aisles back to get some. When I returned moments later the basket was nowhere to be found. Maybe I'd left it in another aisle? I searched the store and at last found another supermarket employee just as she was reshelving my last two items. So, unattended shopping carts were also a capitalist plot. I sighed, returned the eggs and walked sadly and empty-handed out of the store, muttering words better kept to myself than repeated.

I never shopped at the Kaufhalle again, but toward the end of our stay I did return for another reason. I was preparing a photo-essay on life at post for the State Department magazine and decided to photograph an American housewife doing her shopping at the local supermarket. (Readers would never have to know that the author dared not set foot in the store!) I got several shots of the model, bag over shoulder, pushing a nearly empty cart along the aisles before yet another market employee descended upon us to proclaim that it was forbidden to take photographs in the store!

Fortunately she did not confiscate my film. Had she thought I'd have it developed and send it to the CIA? Maybe they would glean some state secrets from it, but as far as I was concerned the Cold War was over and the East German Kaufhalle army had won.

I had many pleasant experiences in East Berlin, some even culinary, but was never again so cocky as to think I could be assimilated into a foreign culture in such a short time as two years. And to this day I take a deep breath before I enter any food store in any country.

Birthday Season on the Other Side of the World

Pat Duffy

It's birthday season for Josh and me - mine's coming up in a few days and Josh had his about ten days ago. Turning a year older makes us feel even more keenly the reality that we have lived, worked and studied in China for nearly a whole year.

On April 21st, Josh's birthday, some friends came over for dinner and we ate long-life noodles, a traditional Chinese birthday custom. We also ate a big, gooey, white icing, pink-rose-covered birthday cake (a western custom adopted by all 'modern-thinking' Chinese of the younger generation).

Birthday cakes in China are almost a caricature of the big, gooey birthday cakes one finds in American bakeries; the Chinese birthday cakes are bigger, gooier and seem to have three times the number of pink icing roses, and the artificial pink color of the roses is so intensely artificially pink, it is like no color found in nature. The effect is a photorealist painter's vision of a birthday cake in three dimensions - more Kodachrome than Kodachrome.

Kodachrome cake was also the centerpiece of Teacher Wang's birthday dinner. Teacher Wang is one of Josh's Chinese language teachers at the university in Nanjing. He's a young, single guy who lives in the university dormitory for young, single male teachers, and he shares his room with three other single academics like himself. It's a small room, and you can't believe that four grown people actually live there together, but they do, as evidenced by the two sets of institutional iron bunk beds and four small desks. The walls are painted institutional beige or green or gray, I'm not sure which.

Amazingly, in this drably painted, tiny crowded room, a big delicious birthday feast was served - all prepared on two electric hot plates in some little room down the hall. I wanted to see just how Teacher Wang and his friends were managing to make all the scores of birthday banquet dishes on two small electric hot plates, and so made several attempts to follow them into the mysterious hot plate area. My attempts were in vain. Each time I tried to follow them out of the room, I was told, "No, Lao Du, you just sit and drink tea!" ('Lao' = old, 'Du' = 'Duffy'). I am told that this 'Lao' is a term of respect in Chinese, often used when younger people address older people. I was first introduced to it by one of my Chinese colleagues who wasted no time in letting me know that since I was older than he, it was proper for him to call me 'Old Duffy' ('Lao Du') and for me to call him 'Young Joe' ('Xiao Zhou'). I wouldn't have this and told him we'd have to compromise about the names - I agreed to call him Xiao Zhou; he called me Pat.

But at Teacher Wang's birthday party, I was addressed with the honorific Lao Du and Josh was addressed as Lao Ke ('Old Cohen') by the ten or so younger guests. We all had a merry time. In the beginning I was afraid that Wang's friends might be uptight having two older foreigners in their midst, but they seemed excited and delighted, and asked us all kinds of questions like, "Is it really true that it's illegal to live in an unheated apartment in the U.S.?" We discussed this question as we all sat around the fold-out dinner table, zipped and buttoned into our winter coats because buildings in China located south of the Yellow River are not heated in the winter, and this was December. The food warmed us up, as did the very sweet wine with which we toasted Teacher Wang and one another. After dinner, everybody got a piece of photorealist birthday cake, which we all consumed, happily clicking our chopsticks.

While eating and talking, I looked at the decor of the room. There was a Chinese version of a pin-up calendar with a picture of a pretty Japanese actress; there were lots and lots of sausages, hanging from strings from the ceiling, apparently meant for decoration as well as consumption; and then, to my very great surprise, there was a crucifix - a big, gaudy, overly shiny brass crucifix hanging on the wall.

"Is someone here a Christian?" I asked.

"A what?" one person responded, thoughtfully stabbing his slice of birthday cake with his chopstick and repeating the English word, 'Christian' as if trying to recall what it meant.

"We are all Chinese," another person offered, hoping to clarify things.

"No," I said. "I know you're all Chinese, but is anyone here a Christian - I mean, believe in the Christian religion?" I said, pointing to the crucifix.

"Oh!" replied Teacher Wang, suddenly understanding and pointing to the crucifix, himself, "You mean, because of it? Oh, no!" he continued, laughing, "It's just for fun!" And then he threw back his head and laughed even more heartily as he stuffed a hefty piece of photorealist cake into his mouth with his chopsticks.

After the birthday, it was time for entertainment. First, a couple of people sang songs - an event you can almost always count on at a Chinese party. We heard a currently popular Chinese love song, and the ever-popular "Edelweiss," from the movie "The Sound of Music," a great hit here.

Chinese birthday parties seem to follow a certain pattern, a pattern that becomes clear after you've attended a number of them. Just about everything that happens at the parties is predictable because everything has been pre-planned. To the Chinese, the western notion of a party - walking into a room full of people, many of whom you don't know, grabbing a drink and strolling about the room uncertainly until you find someone to talk, dance or drink with would be considered an unpleasant use of one's leisure time.

Birthday parties seem especially designed to keep uncertainty to the barest minimum. First, there is no unsure strolling around the room. All the chairs have been arranged side by side along the four walls of the party room. Each person takes a seat and remains there for the duration of the party. Selected persons have been pre-designated to give performances and seated persons have been pre-designated to watch and applaud. At a particular point in the party, there is a clamor for "spontaneous" performances, but generally, everyone knows who will be 'pushed into' performing spontaneously, and those persons have sufficiently prepared themselves in advance.

The performances are definitely a mixed bag - singing, dancing and dramatic recitation, both Chinese and western style, from various periods in history. At one party, two students recited classical poetry together. After the Chinese poetry recitation, a rather large, husky student sang the Italian opera piece "Santa Lucia" (in Italian) in a booming, melodramatic voice. As the song progressed, his voice became more booming and more melodramatic until finally, at the end, he threw his arms wide and bellowed out the final words, "SAN-TA LU-CI-IA!" If any Americans of this student's age had been present, they would have been in hysterics at this sight, so I kept expecting to hear at least a few giggles from the audience. Instead, the Chinese students' faces were filled with dead serious admiration. Thunderous applause followed.

Applause also followed the after-dinner entertainment at Teacher Wang's birthday party. Then the guests splintered off into various activities. Some took part in a boisterous game of cards, two others moved to a corner of a bottom bunk bed for some conversation, another played his harmonica while absently staring at the gaudy crucifix. One performer retired to a corner to study for an exam. While he read, he was unashamedly biting his nails, gnawing at his cuticles, and even "playing piano" on his teeth, moving his fingertips across them and tapping out some imaginary tune - activities generally reserved for those times when one is sure one is alone. People in China get so used to being crowded together all the time that it appears they learn to create their own "psychic wall" when need be, shutting out those around them, and rendering themselves "alone."

As I observed the guests engaged in their various activities, I noticed two young women huddled on a bottom bunk bed, pointing at my feet and giggling helplessly. I looked down at my feet, but saw only my simple Chinese black cloth shoes. "What's funny?" I asked them in my broken Chinese.

"Oh!" they laughed helplessly, now that I'd discovered their private joke, "Your shoes! Nobody in the city wears shoes like that! Only the old peasant women in the countryside wear shoes like that!"

When it was time to say goodnight we thanked our hosts for their wonderful hospitality. We made Teacher Wang promise to attend Josh's birthday banquet, coming up in the springtime, and my birthday banquet coming up a few weeks after that. I announced that at my birthday banquet I wasn't going to have a copy of a western-style birthday cake. I wanted a real Chinese birthday cake, one made of long-life noodles! Our Chinese hosts looked at me uncomprehendingly. Then Josh translated what I'd said into Chinese, but the uncomprehending looks remained. After a silence, Teacher Wang repeated my words in slow English, "You want a birthday cake made of long-life noodles," as if to clarify my meaning for the others and for himself. No sooner had he confirmed what I'd said than the entire group burst into hysterical laughter. Laughter was the music that surrounded us, united us and divided us as Chinese hosts and American guests parted, each marveling at the strange birthday notions that came from the other side of the world.

Latin Hearts

Pam Perraud

It began as a typical glorious Saturday, pleasantly warm but not yet sticky. We had lived in Rio de Janeiro just long enough to know that it would be unbearable in the apartment by lunchtime. Time to get out before the hoards. My French husband and I quickly gathered all of our beach gear and hustled our fidgety kids, our eight year old son Marc and his four year old sister Andrea, into the Alfa and headed for the beaches for relief, like everyone else. Beaches are an institution in Rio. That is where all the action is. But we were not looking for action. We just wanted some peace and quiet as well as respite from the heat. Great day for the beach.

It was eleven by the time we started to snake our way through the heavy traffic on the beach roads in front of Copacabana and Ipanema. The sandy stretches were already thick with bronzed Brazilian beauties. There were also plenty of families already thoroughly settled for the day with blankets, radios and beer. Too many people, too much noise, not enough space for our tastes. We pushed on, trying to get away from the din of the crowds in search of a more peaceful scene.

We were pleased with our luck in finally finding the ideal spot. Perfect...secluded and serene...with enough palms to shade us from the unrelenting sun. We just had to swing the car around to park slightly off the main road.

As we started to unload the car, I was startled to notice a police car silently pulling up behind us from a tiny dirt side road. One of the officers, tall burly fellow, got out of his car and gestured to my husband to stop where he was. Given the fact that the officer looked none too friendly and I had already heard many stories about Brazilian police, I decided to quickly duck back into the car, deserting my husband and hoping that his newly acquired Portuguese would not fail him now. It looked as though he would need it.

They stood at the front of the car. My husband's back was to me but I had a full view of the officer. I could see the sweat starting to roll down my husband's neck. From the few snatches of Portuguese I could understand and from the amount of gestures exchanged, I guessed there was a big problem. Bad day for the beach.

After a few minutes, my husband returned to the car, opened the door and whispered, "Get together all the money you can find, fast."

"What did you do wrong? Was it the U-turn you made?" I said.

With that, my Gallic husband gave me one of his withering you-Americans-are-so-naïve looks. "He says he may have to impound the car...so try to find some more money." Then, he headed back to continue the discussions.

I was shocked. The car! Of course, I should have guessed. The Alfa Romeo was the company car. Too flashy! Damn, why couldn't we have had a little VW bug like everyone else in Rio? Doesn't the company ever think of these things?

Frantically, I enlisted the help of the kids to search for money in, on and under the seats. We looked everywhere. Luckily, they thought it was a game and it kept them busy, but panic started to set in for me. Would they really take the car and leave us all in the middle of nowhere? How would we ever get back home with the kids? Maybe they wanted something else.

As we searched for money, their negotiations continued in the hot sun. As the car sweltered and heated up like a tin can, things seemed to heat up outside, too. Among the candy gum wrappers we managed to glean some cruzieros from all the trash. I surreptitiously passed the few bills and loose change through the window to my husband. He was not pleased by the fruits of our labors. Negotiations continued.

After what seemed ages, my husband shook hands with the officer and returned to the car. He looked relieved, slightly amused when he sat down and started the car. The once menacing officer now nodded and gave him a friendly farewell salute and I wondered what else my husband had bargained away...

I was impressed by my husband's performance. Trial by fire, or in this case, by heat. I knew I never would have known what to do if it had happened to me. I would have panicked. "So, the money worked. I can't believe it. We were really lucky. How did you ever manage?"

My husband only shrugged and smiled saying, "It was a very strange negotiation. Unique in fact. He refused the money at first."

"He actually refused the money? Are you kidding, why?" I couldn't believe it.

"He told me it would not be the honorable thing for him to do to accept the money unless he knew it was coming from the heart. That's why the negotiations took so long. I had to convince him that I only give bribes from the heart."

Latins are different; everything, but everything comes from the heart.

Newcomer

Monica Granqvist

I've just arrived in Belgium and Brussels, my new home! It's only going to be my home country for about two years but, all of a sudden, I'm running into new languages, new customs and a new currency.

My first day starts with a taxi ride, rushing to an urgent appointment. The habit of always being late is one I've brought with me from Sweden, for that's where I come from. First I try to get into the front seat of the car, next to the driver (another Swedish habit). Impossible! The seat's piled up with maps, newspapers, books, pencils, gloves, a pullover, an apple and other handy things. This prompts me to realize that passengers are supposed to sit in the back seat. I place my bag on the seat, walk around the car, get in on the left side and tell the driver where I want to go. He gives me a glance in the mirror and says, in French, "You're from Sweden, aren't you?"

Is my French that bad? I studied it for some six years in school (even if that's history now), practiced it a little from time to time, and read the language - essays, if not thick novels. And before I ordered the taxi, I thoroughly rehearsed the things I wanted to say. And how has he guessed I'm from Sweden? Why not Norway, Denmark, Fiji, Guatemala or whatever?

He gives me the answer himself: "Only people from Sweden put the safety belt on in the back seat." Of course we do, we're drilled that way. It's a reflex! Helmets on when cycling, only buying wine and alcohol in special state shops, and safety belts on as soon as we get in a car...

Some ten seconds after getting into the taxi, I thank my lucky stars that I'm in the back seat. It's the safest place to be. At almost every corner, cars shoot out at high speed from the right, like popcorn heating on a stove. They're claiming their privilege in accordance with the traffic regulation which says something about everybody having priority from the right.

Yes, yes, we do have a rule like that in Sweden too, but we don't use it as a pretext for not casting even a casual glance to the left. The only moments of relaxation come at the major crossroads where all the cars arrive at the same time, everybody blocking everyone else. Forgetting the hooting of all those horns, these moments give me brief relief.

Of course, we reach our destination safe and sound. After all, it's not the first time my taxi driver has driven through Brussels. I look over his shoulder to see the price on the meter, as I'm not sure I've understood what he has said to me, in French of course.

I take out a 100-franc note and give it to him. It seems a very reasonable amount compared with taxi fares in Sweden. Using body language, I try to let him understand he can keep the change (a sign in the car has told me that the tip is included, but I want to show a little generosity by rounding up the sum from 92.7 to a round 100).

He looks puzzled. I make a second attempt to convince him that I don't want the change. A tiny sense of anxiety lurks in my mind. Does he think I'm insulting him? Maybe I've hurt his pride? Now his face turns into a question mark and he blurts out: "*Mais, Madame....*" For the third time I try to make myself clear, using fragments of the French language and pointing to the digital figures on the meter. "*Mais, Madame...* that is the radio!" he explains, and then points to another dial lower on the panel (almost on the floor, I think) which displays another set of figures. "That is the price, Madame!"

I must admit I feel a fool. I blush and fumble in my wallet furiously to find the other 600 francs. The price is 690 francs. That's more like Sweden!

To avoid another embarrassing mistake on the way back, I decide to travel by tram. It takes me a while to understand that, in Brussels, the trams go underground in the center of the city. It's not a real Metro but, in central Brussels, both the trams and the real 'Underground' run on the same tracks. So you get to your tram connection by going downstairs at the Metro sign.

Above ground, the trams behave more like you might expect them to. Some friendly fellow-travelers tell me that tickets are available on the tram itself. You buy them direct from the driver. But tickets can also be bought from special machines at some of the bigger stations.

I could tell you a lot more about the Brussels trams but will refrain from doing so because I'm sure you couldn't possibly be interested. I just want you to understand that I was well prepared for this first trip on a Brussels tram. I even knew how to cancel the ticket (what the French call *compostage*, strangely enough) when I've bought it.

Once on the platform, I place myself in a strategic position so that I can get in at the front door. I have the right amount of money for a five-stop ticket in my hand. The tram arrives, and I stand there like a lemon waiting for the door to open. Nothing happens, so I knock on the door. The driver tries to tell me something.

A passing passenger, who has alighted from the middle door, also says something. As he sees me standing there still knocking he says to me, mercifully in English: "Press the green rubber pad." I look and look. What and where on earth is the green rubber pad? My savior steps forward and puts his finger on a thin strip - it was probably green when it was new - between the two halves of the door. *Et voilà!* The doors open! Once again, I feel 'NEWCOMER" written all over my face.

Best thing to do: buy a car of my own. From intention to action. I know exactly what kind of car I want: a small runabout, just big enough for a Swedish-type shopping expedition. Easy to park. One of the kind that comes to a sudden end metaphorically, as if the factory workers had decided it was time to go home and abandoned the car half-done.

So I go to the dealer. I tell him which make, which model and which color I want (metallic dark-blue). The salesman courteously takes my hand and congratulates me on my excellent choice. The little one will be mine in - wait for it - eight weeks!

And I thought I could just pay for it and drive it back to the garage I've specially rented in the apartment block where I live. All the paperwork has already been solved with a single phone call. But this is just the start of my wait.

Nine weeks later, 'Little Blue' arrives at the dealers, naked. Now the big circus begins. The tax inspectorate, the licensing people, the transport ministry, the insurance company, all want to get involved, in person or by mail. All of them have to apply their official stamp to different papers. At one point it develops into a 'Catch 22' situation: no license plate without insurance, no insurance without the number of the plate.

On Christmas Eve I and my whole family visit the dealer's backyard to wish 'Little Blue' a Merry Christmas. We pat her on the nose and promise to take her home as soon as possible.

At last the license plate arrives at home with the post. With the plate in my bag, I go back to the car dealer. They prepare the second plate, fix the two to the car, and make a final checkup. The salesman and I have become close friends in the meantime, so we take a heartbreaking farewell and I drive off in "Little Blue".

Now I can go by taxi, by tram or in my own little car and feel at ease. And I can at least hope to make people happy without giving them the chance to laugh at my 'newcomer blunders' any longer!

Zut Alors!
It's Nothing Personal!

Constance Leisure

I admit it. I'm a milquetoast, a social creampuff, in a word, gutless. I can't help it, I was raised that way. At the dinner table, my parents never spoke above a civilized murmur. I curtseyed to the nuns in the corridors at school. My brothers called our grandfather "sir." If a friend did something unforgivable, at the very worst, we might stop speaking. But actually voice my displeasure? Never! The art of in-your-face confrontation hadn't been invented.

How odd to move to Paris and find that the wheels turned, the grist of French civilization was made - even those vaunted ideals *Liberté, Egalité, Fraternité* were underpinned - not by centuries of finely polished behavior, Cartesian reasoning, and fraternal feeling for one's fellow man, but by a deep and abiding love of abrasive confrontation.

Waiting in a line one day at the *Palais de Justice* where we'd encountered nothing but rudeness and red tape while trying to establish residency, my husband reminded me of the old vaudeville joke about New York waiters: Man walks into a restaurant, sits down and says, "Waiter, bring me a glass of water and the manager!" He explained that it was the same in France. If you attack first, you'll automatically start out on the right foot. It was nothing personal, it was just the way to behave. I liked the joke, but to actually live by it? I wasn't sure.

I clung to my nice-girl upbringing. Wouldn't politeness carry me through in this most civilized of countries? Unfortunately the quotidian undermined my determination. At the dry cleaners my coat came back looking worse than when I brought it in. "What are these spots?" I asked.

"Madame, we've wasted our time running it through twice already, these stains are permanent."

"But they weren't there to begin with," I said.

"Of course they were. It's impossible to clean," she retorted, shaking my coat like a bulldog. She'd been well trained in the attack.

My new doctor looked me up and down and told me that the mild obesity that is tolerated in America is frowned upon in France. As he took my blood pressure (thank heaven it was predictably low), I promised myself to begin exercising now that baguettes and cheese were a part of my daily diet.

At the hairdressers, I love the person who cuts my hair but the colorist, a brunette who specializes in blond streaks called *mèche*, is not so welcoming. I generally found that I had to wait an average of 30 minutes before she would even deign to approach, and was unfriendly when she finally did. I decided that perhaps it was advisable - as it is at dinner parties in Paris - to come a little late.

"What time was your appointment? Don't you know how busy I am?" were her first words when I arrived the next time ten minutes late. She tossed her shiny chestnut mane and got down to work. "What kind of conditioners have you been using? You don't buy them at the supermarket, do you?" She gave an arch smile, knowing that I probably wasn't using the expensive salon brands. "Your hair is in a terrible state. When was the last time you washed it? It's too clean. I've told you before it's impossible to work with clean hair." She held a strand in the air. It did seem staticky. I wished guiltily that I hadn't washed it. That I used a more satisfactory conditioner. That I hadn't been late. That I could speak up!

Driving through vineyards in the countryside, my husband and I saw a "For Sale" sign on a little house and fell in love. In France, when you buy property, the husband owns it. If he dies it doesn't automatically go to the spouse - indeed, under the law, it must be divided among the wife and other kin. Some widows are unpleasantly surprised when they find that distant cousins become the proud owners of half their property. We decided to buy our house jointly so there would be no problems later.

"We don't do it that way in France," explained the lawyer to my husband, and then, confidentially, "You're asking for trouble. Your wife will make your life miserable if you own it together. If things don't go well, she can cause you a lot of *soucis*." We went to a notary in Paris to sign some preliminary papers. He quizzed us about our choice, clucking with disapproval and shaking his head in obvious confusion and disgust when we insisted.

A few months later, the local notary officiated at the final sale. He telephoned our notary in Paris. "Well, she's here," he said, giving me the once over, and then glancing at my husband with a concerned look. "Yes, we both advised him against doing it this way, didn't we?" he nodded, listening to his *confrère*'s response. "Yes, well, I guess we have no choice but to let him do it. Maybe it will be all right." I gritted my teeth, then smiled politely as I signed the papers.

In Paris, we live in a rented apartment. I have a nodding acquaintance with most of my neighbors, but the only time I have a lengthy conversation with one is when someone complains about a leak, or clanging pipes, or some other unexplained problem which, they insist, must obviously be originating in our apartment as we are on the top floor. It's most often the impeccably dressed blond from the apartment below who insists on coming herself to check on things. She'd look around then tell me to call the plumber, or the manager, or whoever was responsible for repairs. At the beginning, I was unfailingly cordial.

But when my daughter, Clemmie, came home in tears, everything changed. She sobbed that our blond neighbor had called her a *garçon* instead of a *fille* and insulted her dog. Then the harridan grabbed some passing neighbors and enlisted them in further berating my eleven-year-old. Four angry adults against one little kid. It hardly sounded fair.

I pondered the insults and accusations as I comforted my daughter. The woman definitely knows Clemmie is a girl, despite her short, curly hair. The dog, however, may have justifiably aroused some ire. Being a male, he is inclined to lift his leg dangerously close to the flowerbed at the entrance to our apartment building - an action which I've warned my children to beware of. But still, our neighbor didn't have to gang up on a little girl and make her cry. I told my daughter I'd set the woman straight.

I steeled myself. The idea of actually confronting my rather stiff neighbor and telling her to lay off my kid - justifiable or not - gave me discomfort. But it had to be done.

It had always been a cool, formal, *Bonjour Madame* between us, but the next time I stopped her and said, "You made my child cry, why?" She looked a little flustered but quickly responded: "Well, it's that awful dog. *Insupportable!*" I calmly told her that if she had a problem with the dog she should speak to me about it. No one has the right to attack a child. "Attack a child!" she exclaimed, fluttering her hands. "I would never touch someone else's child." I explained that the attack was of the verbal, not physical variety - but it was no less painful.

She pulled herself up. "If you were French you would never have the nerve to speak to me this way," she said. "I know that because you're a foreigner you don't realize what you're saying." I assured her I understood exactly what I was saying.

We had a few more *tête-à-têtes* after that. She was obviously intent on defending herself against my charges. It's nothing personal, I told her, drawing myself up to my full height as she had done.

Now when the pipes clang she doesn't ring my bell. She telephones to tell me she's bringing the plumber and then stands over him while he fixes it. When some renovation downstairs stopped the heat in mid-winter, she made sure ours got fixed at the same time hers did.

I switched dry cleaners, telling the new ones in advance that there might be some potentially difficult spots but that I expected that they would be properly attended to. "*Bien sûr, Madame*," said the attendant. The clothes came back perfect.

I changed doctors, too. My haircutter went to a different salon with a different staff and I followed her. Although she's still adorable, strange to say, the new colorist's personality seems eerily familiar. She fingers my hair with disdain. I feel a stirring within. *Oh waiter, bring me a glass of water and the manager, s'il vous plait.* Nothing personal, of course.

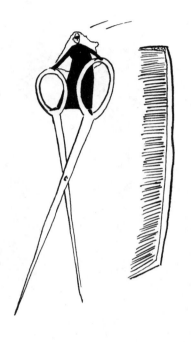

Clipped in Kuwait

Patsy Souza

Changing hairdressers can be nerve-wracking, even if it's only across town. Halfway around the world and in another culture it can be traumatic. When I arrived in Kuwait, January 1992, the country was busy getting back on its feet after the devastation of the Gulf War.

By the time I was in need of a haircut I still hadn't found a beauty shop. I had asked for a recommendation from each acquaintance I made. The answers were always the same, "Before the war..." Desperate, I decided one of the five-star hotels might be the place to go. I called several. "Sorry Madame, not in service yet. In one month," I was promised. Then my luck changed, or so I thought. "Yes, let me connect you," the operator said, giving me hope.

"Halloo?" a male voice greeted me.

Happily booked, I drove to the hotel on the appointed day. Following the receptionist's directions I took the escalator to the hotel's lower floor. High on a wall was a sign, BEAUTY SALOON. I chuckled at the spelling. Grabbing the door handle, I pulled. Nothing happened. I tried again. Realizing it was locked, I walked beyond to a flower shop. "Outside and around to the back," the young Asian woman told me. I walked through unattended gardens to a door propped open with a large can which had the word 'poison' printed on the side. Hoping it wasn't an omen, I opened the door and peered inside. Two young men were washing the hair of some Kuwaiti women.

"Reception?" I asked, looking beyond to a larger room.

Having my hair washed I worried that no one I'd met in the shop, so far, spoke English. With my few words of Arabic and a bit of charades I had convinced them I had an appointment. Seated before a mirror, my wet hair combed back from my face, I watched the young attendant disappear through curtains behind me. Waiting, I glanced in the mirror viewing the women under dryers and at the other hair stations. All Kuwaiti but me. A blonde amongst raven-haired beauties. Dark curious eyes watched me.

"Halloo," a chubby Lebanese man greeted me, reaching for my hair. "Cut?" he asked, watching me in the mirror.

"Trim," I countered, hoping he knew that meant less. I watched as his head cocked to one side, then he ran his hand through my hair again, asking, "cut?" Nervous, I pulled a hunk of my over-grown wedge out from my head. Showing about a quarter inch beyond my fingers, I made clipping motions with my other hand, hoping he realized that's all I wanted cut off. A confused look crossed the full face under the mustache. He hollered for someone. A slight young man appeared, they exchanged words, the hairdresser again running his hands through my hair.

"Yes Madame, what you want?" the younger of the two inquired. Thank God, someone spoke English!

"Please," I said, "a trim." Again I pulled at my hair and cut it with my imaginary scissors. "Then blow dry," I said, using a brush to illustrate the strokes needed to get the smoothness I liked. The two men watched me, then exchanged glances. "Yes, yes," the hairdresser said, convincing me he understood. Feeling a bit more secure, I slid back in the chair. The young interpreter walked away. The hairdresser picked up his scissors. "Cut," he said, getting to it.

I'm not sure at what point I knew things weren't going as I'd hoped - perhaps when I could see my ear where hair had once hung. My gut tightened, but I said nothing. The hum of clippers brought my attention from the sides of my hair to the back. I could feel great quantities of hair falling away and down my neck. On the verge of tears I reminded myself how forgiving my hair had always been and how fast it grew.

Glancing into the mirror, I became aware of two Kuwaiti women watching me being clipped. Rarely do Kuwaiti women have short hair; they must have been shocked at my haircut. They blatantly stared and whispered to each other. I only hoped they weren't saying how bad it looked, but were delighted at the hair mounting on the floor, local tradition being, when your hair is cut, your husband will exchange your shorn locks for gold, ounce for ounce.

The pain of seeing my hair cut, my long worn style destroyed, was nothing compared to the shock of the final product. What hair I had left had been teased, sprayed, and sculptured into nothing like I'd seen before. Leaving the shop angry and embarrassed I fled to my car, worried I'd run into someone I knew. Then I laughed as I checked my reflection in the rearview mirror; who would have recognized me!

The Persian Cats
of Ispahan:
1958

Drusilla Guérin Walsh

In 1958 nothing much had changed in Ispahan since the sixteenth century. Our driver, Mr. Singh, a tall, thin Parsee from India whose reason for being in Iran was never explained, looked as though he belonged there. He wore a turban and one gold earring. He spoke Persian and quite a bit of English. After taking my French husband to work in the morning, he would return to our house in case I needed him to drive me around on errands, which was more fun for me than staying at home while the cook went. On other days Mr. Singh tutored me in the mysteries of the language I would probably never be able to read since the script was Arabic. I wrote everything down phonetically, finding the words rather easy to pronounce except that some were confusing because they sounded like English words but with different meanings. For example, *burro* meant 'to go', *hast* sounded like 'to have' but meant ' to be', and *chap* meant 'left'. However *music* meant 'music' so that was easy, at least until you heard Persian music and then you began to wonder if it really was music.

Mr. Singh appeared one morning and found me in a state. My black kitten, Fel-fel, had disappeared. The cook and I had hunted high and low, and called for him from the flat roof of our house to the back of the garden. No Fel-fel. Mr. Singh had an idea. "We go find him in car," he said. So off we went. Mr. Singh drove with shoulders hunched and head slightly bowed to keep his turban from rubbing against the top of the tiny Citroen. We drove slowly along the gurgling gutter-lined lanes and looked up trees and down alleys. I called and called Fel-fel's name, which means pepper in Persian.

Discouraged after a while, I suggested we drive around the corner to the butcher shop and get something for dinner. Hanging from a hook in the ceiling was a fat shiny carcass sprinkled with flies. There was nothing else in sight, that is, nothing cellophane-wrapped and ready to go. There never was. The indolent flies hardly moved as I pointed to, but did not touch, the part of the back near the bone where the fillet was.

As the stone-faced butcher was carving it out for me, a black kitten wandered in the back door.

"Fel-fel!" I bent down to pick him up. He, however, hissed, raised the fur on his little arched back, spat and ran. The butcher laughed showing a mouth filled with gold teeth. I, anxious to explain, said in my nascent Persian, *"Gorbe siah kuchek hastam, esm Fel-fel, Gomshod."*

He dropped his knife on the marble chopping board, went to the door and beckoned the driver. With his back to me, the butcher repeated in a low voice what I had just said. He sounded upset.

"What's wrong," I demanded. "What did I say?"

Mr. Singh shook his turbaned head and with eyes downcast pulled pensively on his earring for a moment. "Wrong verb," he said sadly. "Very sorry. He tell me you say, 'I am little black cat name Fel-fel. Got lost'."

When Mother Came to Visit

Sandra Reid

M om had been visiting us in London for two weeks when she came to my office to complain about the terrible lunch she'd had at my favorite pub.

"You'd think they could get a hamburger right," she said, slumping into a chair near my desk, ignoring the mounds of proofs spread in front of me. "But this thing was tough as shoe leather. I don't think it was ground beef - it tasted like something you'd feed the dog."

I had warned her about English burgers and recommended the steak and kidney pie, but she'd ignored my advice, just as she'd ignored everything I'd suggested for her visit.

"Pack light," I'd said, when she rang at five a.m. on a Sunday morning to tell us she was coming. "You won't believe how far you've got to haul your luggage." Three or four interchangeable outfits, I'd said. A raincoat, umbrella, and waterproof shoes.

But when David and I met her at Heathrow, she was pulling two large suitcases on wheels and carrying an overstuffed shoulder bag, a camera, and a large purse. A plastic bag holding duty-free cigarettes was tied to the belt of her raincoat. We crammed into the tube. We lugged her bags across Green Park Station, hauled them up the steps at Finchley Road, then fumbled along the uneven pavement a half-mile to the bed and breakfast. She was on a tight budget and didn't want to waste money on a taxi.

"I just couldn't pack enough clothes for three weeks in one bag," she explained, puffing along behind us. "They'd be so dirty after the first week."

"We have laundromats in England, Mom."

"Who wants to do laundry on vacation?"

She didn't like London. Her room at the B&B was too small and too cold and the hostess couldn't make a decent cup of coffee. The adapter and hairdryer I cautioned her not to bring blew up the first time she used them. She smoked both cartons of duty-free cigarettes but wouldn't buy more at the local tobacconists. "Oh, I couldn't smoke English cigarettes," she said, wrinkling up her nose. "I've heard about them."

She had recently divorced my father and was living with a man I'd never met called Bud. She carried photos of him in her purse and frequently pulled them out. "He's so different from your father," she said, thumbing through the photos. "I know you'd like him. It's a pity I didn't meet him sooner in my life. He wants to meet you but he doesn't like to travel. He's over six foot tall, and beds here are so small."

"He's been here before?"

"Well... no...."

"Then how does he know the beds are too small?"

She looked incredulous. "Look at the bed in my room - if Bud were here, he'd have to sleep on the floor!"

We were in Harrods, surrounded by other American tourists who thought this was where the English took tea. I'd told her the Savoy or Brown's Hotel were more authentic, but she'd insisted on Harrods. Now, listening to her talk, I was glad - no one here would take offense at the things she said, or laugh when she pulled out her calculator to convert the cost of our tea into dollars. Everyone else was doing the same thing.

She went to Paris for a weekend. She visited the Left Bank, the Louvre and the Eiffel Tower. But Notre Dame made the biggest impression. "They were selling souvenirs in the sanctuary," she said, scandalized. "And did you know that there are gargoyles all over the church? Gargoyles!" She was astounded. We were astounded that she was astounded. David tried to explain the history of the church, but she shook her head, disbelieving. "Gargoyles are pagan!" she exclaimed. "How can the Catholics allow it? Does the Pope know about this?"

I took her sightseeing on a double-decker bus. The guide was cockney, so I interpreted for her. I thought she was listening, but then, at London Bridge, she said, "You know, your father has an alcoholic personality. He's just like my mother that way. I'm so glad I went into therapy, or I never would've seen I was repeating a pattern of co-dependency."

I looked around, hoping the guide's monologue had overpowered her voice.

She eyed me. "You exhibit a tendency for co-dependency. I know you can't afford it, but I'd be glad to pay for your therapy. You have a lot of unresolved issues."

My face felt hot. "Mom, stop it."

She turned abruptly, as if I'd slapped her. She was silent for the rest of the tour.

Now, listening to her complain about lunch, I was the one who was silent, watching the clock and praying David would leave school early and rescue me from my mother. As soon as he arrived, Mom repeated the story of her lunch disaster and I fled the office.

I ran past an elderly man with a cane, walking downstairs. He wobbled and grasped the handrail, but I scarcely noticed him. At the bottom of the stairs, I burst through the outside door and gulped at the cool London air.

A silver Mercedes-Benz was parked at the curb. The man I'd passed on the stairs exited the building. A chauffeur opened the car door for him.

Behind me, David said, "Did you see who you nearly knocked down the stairs?"

The edge in his voice made me turn. "Who?"

He nodded at the car. "Sir John Gielgud."

The chauffeur opened the driver's door. Under the illumination of the dome light, I saw John Gielgud sitting tall in his seat, frowning and blinking; annoyed, I was certain, with me, the obnoxious young woman who had pushed by him on the stairs.

I clapped my hand over my mouth to keep myself from groaning aloud. How could I have been so rude? So thoughtless? So self-absorbed?...So much like my mother?

As the Mercedes pulled away, Mom said, "Who's John Gielgud?"

David paused. "You'd probably know him as the butler in the movie Arthur."

"Oh," she said. "So where are we going for dinner? I hope to God it's someplace better than that pub."

Subways and Museums

Susan M. Tiberghien

M y 84 year old mother wanted to return to Paris. It would be a short second visit - two days. Mom said that was enough for the museums and maybe Montmartre.

But we arrived the day all the museums were closed. The personnel was on strike, so we headed for Montmartre. Our hotel receptionist said there was a direct subway, and the stop, Abbesses, was lovely.

"There're no muggings in the subways here?" asked Mom.

Muggings? I said no, but double-checked with the receptionist.

The weather was windy, cold, and wet. We took off with one large umbrella. The subway was warm and clean. Twelve stops.

"Do you know how deep we are?" Mom asked.

I had no idea.

"Don't worry, I was just wondering."

We arrived at Abbesses and started up the stairs to street level. We climbed and climbed. A circular ramp, with no exits, going on forever. Armed with our long stick umbrella, we emerged from the underground. Mom called it Metro Abyss.

The loveliness was outdoors. There was a little park, trees turning green, grass and tulips in bloom. Even the rain had stopped. All the tourists seemed gathered on the white steps leading up to Sacre Coeur. We took the funicular and slowly Paris - sleek and shining from all the rain - spread herself out at our feet. Mom looked for a railing and I took her photo, hale and happy, hovering above Paris.

We went to watch the artists at the village square. Mom thought an ice-cream cone would be fun. "But not if it's over a dollar."

I wanted so much to say it was one dollar, but she was sharp at detecting any attempt at slyness. "Susan, how much is it?"

A bit more I said.

"How much more?"

I said three dollars.

She said she would wait to be back in America.

The square sparkled with color. More and more artists appeared, setting up their easels, lining up their paintings. Sunlight dried the sidewalks. We moved slowly from one stand to another.

"Do you want your portrait?" an artist asked, addressing Mom.

"Tell him he should pay me," she said.

The artist laughed.

Mom moved me along with her. "Why'd he laugh? Did he understand me?"

"Mom, he was speaking English to you."

"Well, it didn't sound like it."

The next day, the museums were open, but now the subways and buses were on strike. There wasn't a chance for a taxi. So off we went by foot to the Louvre. Wind whipped around us as we crossed the Seine. The I.M. Pei Pyramid glowed in warm light.

We waited inside for tickets. Only the new Richelieu wing was open. There'd be no second glimpse of Mona Lisa. Crowds were lining up behind us. We took the escalator to the covered court-yards filled with statues - gods and goddesses, wild animals.

"Who are they?" asked Mom.

"Each one?"

"No, not all of them. Just those I tell you."

I was glad only one wing was open.

When we got up to the Flemish painting on the top floor and looked back down to the Pyramid, a line now circled the entire square.

I wondered whether to risk the same line at the Musée d'Orsay. Mom was still game. So onward we went, great-grandmother and grandmother, along the blustery *quai*.

"Isn't this where the book stalls used to be?" Mom asked.

I was holding on to her arm, struggling with the umbrella, and watching out for curbs and puddles and traffic. "They're here, Mom, but they're shut. It's raining."

Mom turned and looked at me, "I know it's raining."

The gods and goddesses were with us. There was no line. At the entrance, I tried to keep the umbrella for Mom to use as a cane. But the guard said no.

"Tell him I walked all the way from Virginia with it."

The guard said he'd make an exchange. "Leave the umbrella and I'll get you a wheelchair."

Mom accepted. Bells rang, doors opened, elevators carried us to the top gallery. This time she was queen. She'd raise her hand and point to the painting she wanted to see. The crowds would back away and I'd wheel her right in front. When the crowds didn't make way, she would clear her throat. Sometimes she went "Beep, beep."

We started with the Post-impressionists, then on to the Impressionists. Going downhill we arrived at the ground level and the Pre-impressionists. I thought it was about my turn to sit and let Mom push. But she didn't agree.

"A grand visit," she would tell everyone afterwards. "When the museums were closed, we did the subways, and when the subways were closed, we did the museums."

Dancing All the Way to France

E. Niessen Davis

It was the early sixties and my husband was assigned to his next post... Paris! Having already experienced several overseas moves, we quickly "settled-in" and embarked upon our marvelous adventures in France.

One of my favorite adventures was with an American friend. We took our daughters to ballet classes.

As Kày and I watched from the sidelines we agreed that this would be a marvelous way to lose weight. We got up our courage - our French was for the grocers mainly - to ask Mademoiselle if she had any adult classes.

When she finally understood, her smile showed surprise and pleasure and, *oui*, indeed, she had a class on Saturday mornings starting at nine, and she would be *enchantée* to have us rendezvous with them.

What we *hadn't* managed to interpret, we discovered, to our horror, the first Saturday. An inkling of disaster seeped through us in the dressing room. We felt it rather odd that men and women shared the same room, but thought liberally, ahhh, the insouciance of the French. We told each other: after all, it's much more sensible to save all the area possible for a large dance space rather than duplicating dressing rooms.

However, when they started rubbing down their legs with all sorts of emollients, binding them up with strips of flannel and putting on jersey leotards, we thought they were taking the lesson exceptionally seriously. Their amusement at our especially purchased corduroy Bermudas and tennis shoes is too painful to discuss.

It soon became clear from hesitant questions and answers from some of the younger members who knew a bit of English, that we had enrolled ourselves in practice sessions for performers of the local branch of the Paris Academie. They were practicing for a forthcoming performance.

Kay and I had only a moment to exchange white expressions of irrevocable catastrophe before Mademoiselle was lining us up on the opposite sides of the treacherously mirrored room, between two of the dancers.

Except perhaps to a very young gymnast, all foot positions in ballet are entirely opposed to nature, if not to gravity itself. And it developed that Mademoiselle's "*un, deux, trois*" from the children's classes got astronomically speeded up for adults; stretch work that followed foot work went on interminably.

Soon I was conscious of a mounting noise, sounding like a high pitched hum, coming from the young man behind me. I saw Mademoiselle glare at him and as I looked sideways in the mirror to see him, red in the face from muffling his honest hilarity, I couldn't help but laugh - and his stifled amusement exploded.

This served as a nice clearing of the air, but my laughing was a mistake in a way because now he became my benefactor, continuously leaving off his own work to "help" me. And, actually, I never tried so hard in my life to do something right because he was so dedicated to my advancement.

When we were supposed to put a foot on the bar, I felt great in the first place for getting my leg up that high without bending my knee. That my foot was sticking straight up in the air was a minor point with me. But my "friend" was right there with a kindly "*Non, non,*" and he took my ankle and cranked my leg around to make my foot lie lengthwise along the bar. Of course, very soon this entire leg had no feeling whatsoever so it wasn't too bad. But his maneuver had caused quite a dip in the left leg which he dexterously straightened with his instep to my kneecap. Whether or not he practiced karate on the side was one of the questions I was too breathless to ask.

A glance across the room showed Kay undergoing a similar stretching assist from Mademoiselle. I hoped it was the lighting and that she wasn't actually turning that green. During a brief respite, Kay muttered darkly, "Wait 'til they're pushing 40 themselves..."

After three hours of this agonizing exercise, during which you can, quite literally, see stars, we prepared to leave. They would go on for several more hours of exhausting work.

We hung in there and could wear clothes two sizes smaller. And later, they accepted us with that special charm the wise reserve for dogged idiots. Kay and I had the wonderful experience of being tutored by a bona fide ballet company.

On opening night they allowed us backstage at the Opera House before they went on-stage. Those sweaty, wool-laden creatures from our class metamorphosed into dazzling ballet dancers. Nobody clapped more passionately than Kay and I from first row, center.

C'est le Parfum

Mary Hanford

The buttons kept popping out of their buttonholes. I had paid a tailor 10,000 Central African Francs to make a running suit out of pink and brown African batik, and he had screwed up the buttonholes.

I fussed to myself again, putting the tiny brown ceramic knobs into the slits, standing, then yelping when they slid out again. Nothing worked in Africa, not even my body. For instance, how could I have grown a belly when there was so little snack food available? It was the "patisseries" that beckoned when I returned home from school, and no one came to see me. I lay on the bed and cried.

Later, I sat up and stared at the shelf of my stomach. I pinned the buttonholes so gaps were less likely, splashed on cologne bought from a Paris street vendor and left to join the Hash.*

As I jogged, I looked down once or twice to see if the pinned buttonholes were together, then forgot them in the excitement of keeping up.

Usually at the rear of the runners, I ran in the middle this time. Most could not speed in the heat. Around me ran Americans, Cameroonians, French, Syrians. I fantasized us as a United Nations delegation which was, at last, getting something done - reaching a finish line, if we could only find which trail led to it. Everybody looked sweaty, straggling, mud splattered.

At one point, the jungle broke into a large clearing. Having been running single file, we spread out. In the clearing stood

---

* Hash: a term for Hash House Harriers, which is, in Cameroon, a bi-monthly run along a trail set by other Hashers which is rigorous and tricky. Each Hash is followed by a party, which in Cameroon is called an "On-On". The Hash is an international institution begun somewhere in the British Empire, perhaps in India, spoofing "Only Mad Dogs and Englishmen" to run in the noonday sun. Currently there are Hash runs all over the world.

a small village; about ten compounds of several buildings each. We swarmed like gnats upon the village.

Cameroonian villagers were used to crazy internationals running in the heat. Often small children would clap. Old women shelling beans would cackle.

As we approached, we huddled closer so as to run as directly through the village as we could. I was in the middle of a large group, which was almost walking because of the heat and compounds. We were through most of the village when a thunderous voice boomed in a local dialect. A Cameroonian Hasher* said we'd better stop. We halted at the village outskirts.

A tall, thin man in traditional robes strode towards us. His face and arms looked middle-aged. He carried a staff, but did not lean upon it. Several younger men and a few children walked with him. The young men wore simple brown or bleached robes, but around their waists hung scabbards on rope belts. The Cameroonian who had warned us to stop went up to the thin man and greeted him with palms up, the way one salutes a chief.

They spoke for a while. The Cameroonian translated the dialect into French for the French Hashers who then laughed.

Some other Hashers had walked up to the chief. Now everybody was speaking in French. The chief pushed through the Hashers and walked towards Tony, an American Embassy security guard, and the Cameroonian. The chief's companions walked near him, as if they were bodyguards, their muscles tense and faces stern. The other Hashers hurried towards us.

When the Fon* reached us, one of the young boys ran off and reappeared with a wood stool with lizards and serpents

---

* Hasher: anyone who runs a Hash or who participates in any way in its madness, ie: setting the trail, getting refreshments.
* Fon: a Cameroonian term for a local prince.

carved in its base. The Fon sat down and held his staff like a scepter. He spoke to the men with him. One of his minions stepped forward and began talking in French.

After lively discussion, the Cameroonian Hasher said to me in English, "He wants to marry you. He says he is rich, head of the village and can do as he pleases. You will be taken care of and have a good life. He has other wives who can share the work."

Frightened, I huddled in the center of the now protective Hashers. Three buttons had slid beyond their safety pins.

"There you are," said Tony. "Fixed for life!" He laughed. "What do you say?"

I shook my head. The Cameroonian Hasher told the chief's spokesman that I refused. More discussion followed, then loud talking. The Cameroonian Hasher turned to me and said, "He wants to know who is in charge of you, why you are such an obstinate woman. He says that whoever is in charge should be glad to be rid of an obstinate woman."

The Hashers laughed, and the chief took this as a sign of approval. He rose from the stool and moved towards me. The circle of Hashers tightened.

"Are you certain you refuse this chief?" the Cameroonian Hasher asked me.

I nodded. Three French Hashers animatedly told the chief and his party to leave. Although I didn't understand the answering dialect, the villagers' stiffened bodies and narrowed eyes said "*You* leave. It's our village!"

Everyone started yelling and gesturing angrily. One of the French gave him a version of the "bird," and a chief's guard put his hand on his sword. Tony, who had once worked as a carnival barker, stepped away from me and towards the bargaining party. He and the Cameroonian Hasher talked a long time, the Hasher interpreting to the chief. Tony gave the chief two bottles of aspirin, some matchbooks, and a first aid kit that came with his security guard uniform and that he always took with him on Hashes.

The Chief and party, plus the others, began to joke a little. Finally, Tony said, "Why did you want her anyway?" The Cameroonian Hasher translated for the chief, then again for us.

"*C'est le parfum*," the Cameroonian Hasher said, "And a certain *je ne sais quoi*. He says she doesn't look like many Americans, polished like a table, put together with pegs. She looks like she could unravel. That plus her perfume made him crazy. But he says he doesn't really want an ungrateful woman. She would be too much trouble. She should be glad he wanted her."

The Fon and his companions turned back towards the village, the first aid kit swinging from a bodyguard's rope belt. After smoking some cigarettes and chatting, the runners began the Hash again, eager to get to the On-On, the after-Hash party.

When I got home at midnight, I hurled my muddied running suit over a chair. Those recalcitrant buttons gleamed in the electric light. Some of the buttonholes' binding had frayed, even unraveled. But I had not.

Love, Marriage, and All That Paperwork

Elizabeth Joseph-Mosely

I am now officially a Married Woman. Worse still, I am a Married French Woman. Well, not exactly French, since it appears it will take me 2, 5 or 7 years to earn my French nationality, depending on which demon-spawn of a civil servant I encounter at the *mairie* (city hall). No one seems to know how long it will take, French bureaucracy being an amazingly inexact science.

I had never had any particular desire to get married, but then I never planned on falling in love with a Frenchman. And with my student visa about to run out (and no date of expiration stamped on my relationship), my boy-friend Pierre and I decided the easiest solution to the visa problem would be to get "M"-ed.

Little did we know.

The first step on the road to wedded bliss was to go to the *mairie* of the 9th *arrondissement* (hereafter to be known as the Mairie-from-Hell) to find out about the procedure. I was given a dossier longer than my senior thesis explaining which papers we would need to hand over, and in what order. Although the list was substantial [including birth certificates, translations of birth certificates, certificates of divorce (his) and certificates of celibacy (mine)], we could choose a date after depositing our medical certificates.

Pierre and I dutifully went to see our doctor, who, after describing his Provence vacation for ten minutes and then charging us 400 francs ($80), happily signed off on our physical health. I returned to the *mairie* with the certificates and a list of ideal dates, only to be informed by the administrator (hereafter known as the Wicked Witch of the 9th) that she, in fact, needed all the papers on the list before we could choose a date, because I am an... *étrangère* (foreigner).

Only after I delivered all the documents would the dossier be sent upstairs for approval by a Higher Power (namely the 3rd assistant mayor). I pointed out that her colleague had assured me that only the medical certificates were necessary before choosing a date, and showed her the relevant paragraph in my dossier. "But obviously," she sniffed. I was unaware that the law gave her the power to decide which papers were necessary before proceeding.

I have since learned that her assertion is not *tout à fait vrai*, a phrase which in itself reveals a lot about the French notion of truth. As far as I can tell, there are several levels of truth at work here, ranging from "almost always completely true" to "normally true" to "not really true at all... except." The French don't like to close off their options, which may be why they boast 72 different kinds of bottled water and twelve different words to describe a chicken.

After ten fruitless minutes of arguing with the Witch (how do you say "life-sucking troll" in French?), I knew I was beat. I then began the tedious and expensive process of collecting the necessary certificates, translations and identifications, all of which had to be dated within three months of the wedding. Of course, since no one could tell me how long it would take to approve our file, it was possible that all the papers would expire before we received the OK, meaning we would have to start over.

After several weeks, I returned to the *mairie* and was greeted by a slightly friendlier, if no more helpful, bureaucrat who checked through my mountain of papers, and sadly informed me that the *Certificat de Coutume*, a document that explains the exotic marriage customs in the U.S.A., was missing. I explained that the American Consulate does not furnish that paper, which is not mandatory, anyway. But for the Mairie-from-Hell, it was absolutely essential, so I returned to the Consulate for an official paper stating they do not deliver that official paper.

The certificate of non-deliverance did the trick, and our file was finally ready for inspection. The less-Wicked Witch took all my papers and wrote up the publication of the *Bans* (misspelling my fiancé's name despite the fact it was listed five times on every paper). With the publication of the *Bans* prepared, the file could go upstairs for approval. But wait! On the list of witnesses, I had described someone's profession as *cadre* (salaried). It appears *cadre* is not a sufficient description of someone's job and I was forced to return home, depressed and dateless.

I returned to the *mairie* armed with the exact professional titles of all my witnesses, and the file was finally sent along for approval. A week later I phoned to check on its progress, and was astonished to find that the file had already been approved... except. Except, my student visa was about to expire, and I could not get married without a valid renewal. Surely not all the Americans that get married in France have a valid student visa before taking the plunge? A complex and profound question, destined to go unanswered, since I absolutely could not choose a date until I gave them a copy of a valid student *carte-de-séjour* (and what was I getting "M"-ed for?). So after obtaining my renewal (a story far too long and ugly to recount here), I was finally allowed to choose a date for my wedding.

The young adjoint mayor who performed the ceremony seemed singularly concerned that I have many babies for "La France." He happily handed over my new *livret de famille* which includes space for eight additions to the family. I couldn't even come up with names for eight children, much less give birth to them.

After the wedding, I was even able to take a two-week honeymoon from French bureaucracy before starting the process of obtaining my residency permit. And although I had to wait an hour in a tiny police station in order to *make an appointment* with the main police station, this time, I revel in the knowledge that, at last... my husband had to go, too!

Her Name's Victoria

Susan Reynolds Baime

"Her name's Victoria." I've told this story often. "What else would you call a girl-child born a subject of Her Britannic Majesty?" I could have called her Elizabeth; but "Victoria" speaks to me of Empire, of slow-paced graciousness and more than a little fantasy.

My daughter was born in Barbados, part of the British Commonwealth of Nations. Elizabeth II, by the grace of God, is Queen of Barbados. For a mother from the New Jersey suburbs and a father from small-town Wisconsin, having a baby in Barbados was part fantasy, part adventure and a lesson in how a different culture approaches a universal experience.

During our two-year assignment in Barbados, we knew many expatriate women - American, Canadian, British - who had babies. Most, however, chose to go "home" for the actual birth. Not me! Determined not to be an Ugly American, I would have my baby in Barbados. Barbadian women did it all the time; surely the process didn't vary by location. I would be the sophisticated expatriate, able to cope.

While medical facilities in Barbados were not as up-to-date as those back home, local obstetricians and pediatricians were trained in the U.S. or Britain. I was confident all would be well and only a little "different."

Nothing was very different at first. I saw the doctor regularly, made a reservation at the hospital, lined up a pediatrician. Just like home. I also got a copy of Dr. Spock so I could double check what to expect with my baby.

But differences became apparent as my pregnancy advanced.

Amniocentesis wasn't done, but it wasn't needed. Barbadian women could tell the sex of my baby by looking at my stomach. More than once I was stopped on the street or in a store and asked, "How's that little boy?" The first time, I looked around to see what child was meant, but they meant the child I was carrying. My insistence that I would have a girl was laughed at and chalked up to first-time mother's ignorance. "Boys stand up straight," our housekeeper explained. "That baby's standing right up. He doesn't care what you think."

On one visit to the doctor, I received a list of what to bring with me to the hospital. It was a very long list: nightgowns for me, clothes for the baby, diapers for the baby, sanitary napkins, soap. Didn't the hospital supply any of this? No, I was on my own. Women in the U.S. pack a suitcase for the hospital; I packed a trunk.

Finally, my due date came. No baby. Another week passed. Still no baby. "Enough," the doctor said. "We'll induce you."

I presented myself at the hospital for the real adventure. I was not yet in labor. Or was I? After the induction procedure, two nurses discussed my case. "She didn't need to be induced. Totally unnecessary. She was having mild contractions when she walked in here."

Nurses criticizing the doctor's decision? In front of the patient? This never happened in Summit, New Jersey!

In the U.S., childbirth may have been a doctor-controlled medical procedure, but in Barbados it was a "woman-thing." Yes, a male doctor officially presided (at least for expatriates), but female nurses, midwives, and aides were really in charge. And they made no effort to clarify their rank. Whatever their training or expertise, they were all women helping other women have babies. The professional midwife was as likely as the aide to pour the breakfast cornflakes, offer ice to the woman in labor or mop up a spill.

The delivery room boasted shiny metal equipment and acres of sterilized sheets. Doctor and nurses wore masks and surgical gowns. But the windows were open and without screens. The soft breeze felt soothing, but a small moth flew over my head. Had he been sterilized? Was I the only one who saw an inconsistency here? Yes, as a matter of fact, I was.

Early next morning, a nurse came in, looked briefly at my sleeping daughter and cheerily told me, "You'd better get up and give her a bath."

Get up? Me? I just had a baby! Don't I need rest? And bathe the baby? I couldn't do it. I *knew* newborns shouldn't be bathed. My mother said so; my mother-in-law said so; Dr. Spock said so. Bathing was dangerous. Were these people crazy? Didn't they care about my baby?

But the nurse thought I was crazy. My protests about the danger of infections were not taken seriously. "You Americans," she laughed, "You worry so about germs!"

I noticed other new mothers bathing their babies. And the babies survived. Could the fear of bathing be an American quirk? Dictated by culture and not a law of nature? I worked up my courage and bathed my baby. No ill effects! She even liked her bath!

My husband arrived to take us home. I waited for the nurse to bring a wheelchair. Everyone leaves a hospital in a wheelchair. Not in Barbados. A healthy new mother could just walk. This healthy new mother could walk down three flights of stairs. The hospital elevator was out of service.

Our departure from the hospital was consistent with the entire experience. Mother and baby were cared for. Enthusiasm for the new little person was strong. But childbirth was all a routine part of life. Babies arrive. Moths fly around. Elevators break down. The attitude was warm, relaxed, not-totally-scientific, decidedly unAmerican. "Don't worry so much," one of the nurses said in farewell. "Enjoy the baby."

And we did. Once home, our housekeeper immediately inspected the baby. This really was a girl! "I'll never argue with a mother again," she said, "but this baby sure looked like a boy!"

Her name's Victoria. She acts a bit like a queen on occasion. "She comes by it naturally," I explained. "She was born a subject of Her Britannic Majesty."

A Child Belongs to the Village

Paula S. Gormly

He must have disappeared while I was practicing my rusty Japanese with a tour group of retirees from Yokohama. I was busy making some point concerning Hong Kong real estate ("Prices here are almost as bad as Tokyo!"), turned away from the beach to point out my apartment complex with its numerous amenities and stunning view of the South China Sea when I noticed that my fourteen-month-old was no longer taste-testing sand at my feet.

My husband and I were, by this point in our stay, quite comfortable with our son regularly being picked up and included in complete strangers' photographs of Hong Kong. Undoubtedly the folks back in China or Japan or Malaysia or wherever would get a kick out of their compatriots cavorting with one of Hong Kong's truly exotic offerings: a blonde, green-eyed laughing baby boy.

It didn't really bother us that people were constantly touching his hair, pinching his cheeks, poking his belly. It didn't seem to bother *him*, and on the off-chance that we did have a language in common, Ben was quite the ice breaker. Much more annoying was the stream of *gweilos* ("foreign devils", like us) who would assure us, with an air of enlightened authority, that it was good luck in Asia and especially in China to touch someone with blonde hair. It was also good luck for the person who was being touched. These potentially conflictual events were, in fact, the steppingstones of intercultural communication, and on and on. My husband and I congratulated ourselves on our cultural sensitivity and continued to share Ben and his hair with assorted Hong Kong dwellers and visitors.

While intercultural poster boy was one thing, kidnapping was quite another. I scanned the beach with increasing panic; our little guy couldn't get all that far by himself. How many times had we ex-pat moms talked about how safe Hong Kong was for our kids. Sure, terrible things did happen, but generally not to us. OK, there were things you wished your kids had here (say, a patch of grass to run on), but, at least in our case, maybe the apartment complex's two swimming pools helped make up for it? Perhaps Ben was headed towards the McDonald's because, despite having been born in Paris and having lived his short life in Melbourne and Hong Kong, he really was an American boy, wasn't he?

Arms flapping and tears welling, I ran up the beach and toward the Golden Arches. What would I do, where was a police officer, what would Ben's grandparents say? I didn't like to think how the media could exploit the theme of "privileged *gweilo* mom leaves exclusive ex-pat sanctuary and loses child on the beach below." A woman emptying garbage cans spied me and my distress. "Beybey?" she asked, her face betraying no emotion. "Yes, beybey!" I replied, feeling very hopeful and making a mental note to seriously upbraid the next new arrival who whined about how *no one* in Hong Kong spoke comprehensible English. She pointed at a rather gaudy temple and tourist stop dedicated to the goddess of the Sea, Tin Hau, about a hundred feet down the beach. "Beybey," she smiled. "Beybey, yes, thank you," I shouted. Hopefully, 'beybey' isn't Cantonese for 'discount drinks,' I thought as I sprinted towards the temple.

Somewhere between fear and fury, I entered the large cupola adjoining the temple. Cultural and linguistic differences be damned, I thought. Today I would make my feelings known and someone would be held accountable. In the far corner, I saw a knot of elderly Chinese women crouched around someone who, just maybe, could have been mistaken for a minor temple deity. Relief washed over me.

Half-eaten shrimp cracker in one paw, Mickey Mouse keychain in the other, Ben looked over at me with a small raised eyebrow which seemed to say, "Oh, Mom, what are you doing here?" Almost immediately, his gaze returned to the source of shrimp crackers, which he continued to stuff in his mouth as he happily surveyed his supposed supplicants. I drew nearer, but, unsure of how to engage the group, I stopped a few feet away, arms crossed, observing the scene. I could feel the anger subsiding and thought of the futility of lecturing these women, in English or any other language, on the fine points of child abduction etiquette. Everyone was having such a good time, I just couldn't bear to ruin it.

An older man appeared next to me and asked me if I was Ben's mother. I nodded, silently noting that there were no other likely candidates in sight. "You are worried," he said to me. I told him that I hadn't known where Ben was. "Oh, he is with us," the man replied, as if this was all the explanation I required. Before I could say anything more, a group cackle and cries of agreement emanated from the circle of wizened faces, followed by a generous dose of prodding, poking and pinching directed at Ben. The man next to me laughed as well. "What did they say?" I asked. "They say your son looks just like her grandson," he said, pointing to a very short, plump Chinese granny with gold teeth, jet black hair and dark brown skin. "Oh *really*?" I said, slightly incredulous. "Yes," he said, "he looks so smart."

I still wonder if that was an actual translation or merely a successful attempt to win me over. Any residual annoyance was put aside as I coordinated yet another East-meets-West photo shoot. We then waved our new friends onto their bus and started on our way home. This time, one of Ben's little hands was firmly clamped in mine, the other one was clutching the Mickey Mouse keychain that, I had been told, Ben simply could not do without. I noted that the pocket on the bib of his overalls held one small shrimp cracker for the road. Somehow, I never did manage to find out how Ben had been spirited away from me nor if anyone had actually intended to return him. I did learn a lot more, though, about what constituted a whole lot of fun for Ben and for some elderly residents of a remote Hong Kong housing complex.

I'll admit, there are times when the attention Ben receives can be daunting. But, I also cherish the contact, the smiles, nods, waves and attempts at communication that have come as a result of people's interest in him. There is, I am told, an old Chinese saying, "a child belongs to the village." It's nice, in this increasingly impersonal age of world wide webs, megacities and mass tourism, that a smiling child can still bring the global villagers a bit closer together.

A Wife Who Knows
How To Pack

Sarah Prince Colton

One of the most endearing and maddening qualities of the French is their passionate attachment to personal independence coupled with a fierce loyalty to France and all that is French. When these qualities clash, the pyrotechnics are as brilliant as any Bastille Day fireworks display. One such memorable spectacle took place on a July 1st, as I set off on vacation with my French husband, three daughters, dog, and my father who was visiting from America.

Daddy is an excellent traveler. He travels light and whatever happens is fine with him. If it was not planned, so much the better. My husband, Pierre, also travels light and is an excellent traveler, *if* the food is excellent and served at the appropriate times. On this particular departure day, I was not traveling light. We were leaving Paris to spend the two months of summer vacation at our house in the Loire Valley. Our luggage included clothes for the four seasons (freezing rain is not unheard of in July), in addition to the usual things families take on vacations. Not quite so necessary, I will admit, was the picnic lunch. Pierre does not care for picnics, and we were planning to eat *en route* in his favorite restaurant in Orléans. I had packed it 'just in case,' knowing that even in the land of the best restaurants in the world, things do not always turn out according to plan.

It was 11 a.m., and the plan was to drive an hour and a half to Orléans, have lunch, and then continue to our house near Loches. Although I had calculated that I could endure the two-and-a-half-hour trip with the picnic lunch on my knees, we were more crowded than I had imagined. Since Daddy was with us, I had to ride in the back with the girls and our dog, Julietta, clawing her way back and forth across our bare legs.

July 1st is the worst day (along with August 1st) to leave Paris on vacation. Parisian families crowd onto the same highway on the way to relax for the summer. In addition to the extra traffic created by the holiday season, this year many roads

163

were barricaded by striking French farmers who were in a state of Gallic rage over recently changed European Union rules. Before we had driven ten miles, the traffic was at a standstill. Pierre had told me that he sympathized with the farmers, and during our first fifteen minute wait, he explained the situation with great eloquence and lucidity to my father and the girls.

The second time traffic stopped we waited half an hour. To make matters worse, the engine in our 12-year-old BMW tended to overheat and the only way to keep it from doing so was to turn on the heater inside the car, which according to Pierre, drew heat away from the engine. Everybody sat in strained silence, enduring the heat and watching Pierre smoke. The third time we stopped, it was one o'clock. Pierre asked me how late they served lunch at the restaurant, and when I told him three o'clock, he simply stared glumly out the window. Two minutes later, however, he banged his hand on the steering wheel and shouted, "I'm 'ungry!" It was unclear whether he had said 'hungry' or 'angry,' but we all understood what he meant. He then began cursing the farmers.

"This is scandalous..." he shouted, and then launched into a tirade which contradicted point for point his prior support of the farmers.

Fifty yards down the road we could see the last exit before the toll booth.

"Why we don't leave zis beeg 'ighway and take ze leetle roads. Ze farmers, zey cannot block every road in France. We weel outweet zem, Henri," Pierre addressed my father. "Look at ze map and find me Bièvre. Then see where is most shortest roads to Orléans."

When the traffic finally started moving again, we headed for the exit ramp, and felt a welcome breeze as we sped up to a brisk 40 mph. Our triumph was short-lived, however, as several hundred other cars had made the same decision we did.

Fifteen minutes down the road, the traffic stopped again. The only difference was that now we were on a two-lane road. In the distance we could see an ominous cloud of smoke rising above the line of traffic. Pierre got out and walked up the line of cars to see if he could find out what was going on. My father, binoculars in hand, clamored out, and gazed around at the sight.

Smoke was rising from a barricade of tractors and burning bales of hay about a half mile up the road. When the traffic started moving again, I could see a narrow opening through which one car at a time was allowed to pass. Some people waved gaily as they drove through, others made menacing and rude gestures, shouted out of their windows or blasted their horns. There was a curious mixture of moods among the farmers, as well. Some, with angry faces, were standing around in little groups, while others were laughing as they barbecued meat on grills placed on the tops of bales of hay. Having heard Pierre praise and curse them within the same half-hour period, I decided that a noncommittal smile would be the best policy when our turn arrived.

Once through the eye of the needle, and away from the heat of the fires, we sped through open country for about half a mile before we saw the line of cars stopped in front of yet another barricade. The children groaned.

"Welcome to France, Henri," my husband said with a half laugh. "Are you not 'appy zat your daughter is married with a Frog?"

Pierre opened the car door to cool off the inside.

"I am h'ashamed of my country, Henri," he said. "Look at thees beautiful land. Every-sing to making people 'appy. But no, ze French is h'always complaining about some sing. I am depressing when I sink h'about zis beeg mess."

Suddenly, out of the heat, we heard a lone engine turn on, and another car about three up from ours whipped into reverse, did a partial U-turn, and disappeared down a country lane.

"Do you think that person knows a short cut?" I asked from under the picnic.

"Thees car, she 'as ze license plates of Paris," Pierre said, the fatigue showing in his voice.

"How do you know he doesn't have a vacation house around here?" I asked.

"You are sinking we should follow heem?" Pierre asked in disbelief.

"Why not?" I said, "If he does know something, we might still make it to 'Les Pieds dans L'Eau' in time."

The mention of food galvanized Pierre into action. He quickly maneuvered the car around, and we were off in pursuit of the mystery car. Behind us, we heard the engines of other cars starting, signaling that the traffic was beginning to move again. When we looked around we discovered to our amazement that they were following us!

After a couple of quick right and left turns, the lead car jogged left, the wrong way down a one-way street, and headed down an even smaller road.

"My wife, she ees very clever, n'est-ce pas, Henri?" Pierre said. "Zees man he know where he ees going." Our spirits lifted at the thought of outwitting the farmers and having an adventure, to boot. It also helped that since we were driving faster, the car was no longer overheating, and Pierre could turn off the heater. At the next intersection, the lead car hesitated a moment before making the turn.

"What you sink?" Pierre asked. "Do zis guy knows where ze 'ell 'ees going, or what?"

The pavement stopped and we began bumping down a dirt road which quickly became a heavily rutted grass road running between open fields. Behind us, glimmering in the afternoon sunshine, and throwing up an enormous cloud of dust, was a parade of ten or fifteen cars. At the top of a hill, the car in front of us came to a halt.

"I am going to asking zees man if he know where he ees," said Pierre, jumping out of the car. My father followed. Pierre arrived at the other car, exchanged a few words with the driver, then burst out laughing as the other man staggered laughing from his car.

"Why are they all laughing?" the girls asked me.

"Because we are totally lost," I said, laughing myself.

Since I was laughing, the girls began laughing too. The drivers of the other cars came walking up to the front, and everybody began laughing, talking, gesturing, and pointing in various directions.

My father jogged back to the car, his body and face contorted with laughter.

"Nobody has any idea where we are," he laughed. "Apparently, our lead driver just got fed up and decided to go off on a hunch."

When Pierre got back to the car, Daddy was elated.

"That is the funniest thing I have ever seen," he said to Pierre. Pierre smiled and started the car.

At the top of the hill we came to a small village. A group of old men were playing *boules* in the dust of the lone intersection. The sound of twenty cars converging on their cross-roads interrupted the quiet of their afternoon, and they gazed at us as we drove up. Daddy, checking his map through a magnifying glass, asked Pierre, "Did you say it was Corbreuse that we were looking for?"

Pierre pulled off the road, allowing the other cars to pass, and he and Daddy converged over the map. Out of the window I watched the villagers' grey heads rotate in unison as they followed the movement of each car as it approached the intersection, paused a few seconds and then turned right or left. There were a few waves and toots of good-humored farewells from the drivers, the familiar sounds of the gears shifting, and the cars disappeared into the distance. Within two minutes the noise and dust had settled and the village was quiet again. The group of men resumed their game of *boules*, and the only sound was the intermittent clacking of the balls.

Pierre checked his watch. It was exactly three o'clock. The back of his neck was gritty and sweaty, and his eyes were tired. My heart went out to my tired French warrior, and I thought the moment might be right to mention the picnic.

"You know, Pierre," I began, "I thought we would be having lunch in Orléans, but I brought food for dinner tonight," I paused, and when he did not break in, I added, "We could have it for lunch instead, that is, if you wouldn't mind picnicking...."

Pierre's eyes in the rear view mirror brightened momentarily, then narrowed again in suspicion.

"What kind of sings did you bring?" he asked.

"Let me see," I said. "Cold ham, and onion tarte, deviled eggs, duck paté, salad, garlic sausage, a few baguettes, some brie, chocolate cake...a couple of bottles of rosé...."

"Ees zee rosé cold?" He interrupted.

"Yes, I believe it is," I said.

In an instant, Pierre started the car, and asked into the rear view mirror, "Anybody not for ze idee of a peek-neek?"

A chorus of "No's" erupted from the back seat.

We had a number of inviting side roads from which to choose, and within ten minutes we were spreading our blanket in the grass beside some peaceful tributary of the Loire. My father drank a toast to the farmers, and Pierre drank a toast to his wife, who knows how to pack.

The OJ Simpson Method

Debra Gawron

News events are often used in language classes for purposes of vocabulary and discussion. In this case, the news event became the entire language course.

I was sitting on the roof garden of a hotel in Rome when I first read about the murder of OJ Simpson's ex-wife. I was eating a mortadella sandwich and drinking a glass of chianti, browsing through the *International Herald Tribune*, when I noticed the small item. I hadn't thought about OJ Simpson in years and wasn't particularly interested. I put down the paper to watch the sun setting behind St. Peter's.

I was alone in Rome. My husband had come for a long weekend. He had gone back to Paris that day because he was enrolled in an intensive English course and didn't want to miss classes. He's French and we had always lived together in France, but we had decided that we could use a change and were moving to Miami that summer. I had lived in Europe for ten years and never been to Rome. I wasn't leaving until I did. So there I was, with one of the continent's most splendid cities spread out around me, and I was thinking of all that I had to do to leave it all behind and go back to my homeland, a place I eagerly left behind during the Reagan years. Would I find it changed?

A few weeks later, I was sniffing and wiping away tear-smeared mascara from under my eyes while my charter flight to Miami taxied away from the gate at Charles de Gaulle. It was July and the plane was filled to capacity with French people going off on vacation. Their joyous mood only intensified my sadness at saying good-bye to Paris and also, briefly, to my husband. I was going on ahead with a list of things to do that read: Find a place to live, buy a car, buy a computer, get a job.

I rented a car and checked into a hotel in an area where I hoped to find an apartment to sublet during south Florida's slow summer tourist season. The two gay guys who rented me my room asked me, "So, do you think OJ is guilty?" I hadn't thought about OJ Simpson much and was only vaguely aware that he was now the prime suspect in the double murder. My lack of an opinion on OJ amazed and startled them. Everyone had an opinion on OJ. It had become the national pastime.

This was especially true on TV. The talk shows, which seemed to be as numerous as *boulangeries* in Paris, were brimming with OJ chat. By the time my husband got there a month later, pre-trial motions were in full swing and CNN was broadcasting live from the court room. My husband's first impressions of America were dominated by OJ - and he had never seen a football game in his life.

Within six weeks of my arrival in Miami, I had completed everything on my short but formidable to-do list and started a job, leaving my husband home alone every day with OJ. While I had learned French at the Alliance Française, reading Maupassant, Flaubert and Sartre, he was learning watching the OJ trial on CNN. I was pleased that his shaky English was improving (that intensive English course in Paris was only a small step in the right direction), but he was developing a curious vocabulary. The word *motion* to him had nothing to do with physics but was an argument a lawyer made in front of a judge. While playing tennis on a hot day he said, "Let's take a recess." If he disagreed with me he said, "I object." My husband didn't know whether OJ Simpson had played offense or defense, but he knew all the members of OJ's trial defense team and was becoming an expert on the game rules of the court room.

The debate as to whether or not the televising of the OJ Simpson trial was a good thing to do will go on for a long time. For me personally, I look at my husband and think, it worked for him. He knows more about the American legal system than I ever knew about the French justice system. And he probably learned more about Americans' collective psychology in those first few months than I was able to figure out about the French in ten years. America was defining itself in relation to OJ Simpson. What's positive about Americans came out: our passion for freedom of speech, our willingness to tread on new ground, our openness. But our sore spots showed up too: our racism, our desire to win at any cost, our addiction to television, our delight at a juicy media frenzy. OJ Simpson provided a subject, a forum and a catalyst to bring out all that was good and bad and put it on TV for everyone to see.

To my husband, though, it was better than grammar books and *dictées*. It was like one long dialogue he couldn't stop listening to, except, maybe, during the tediously detailed DNA analysis phase. And it was also good for conversation. At my office Christmas party he could hold his own with anyone on the subject of OJ Simpson, amazing my colleagues with his command of multi-syllabic legal terms. Little did they know that if someone had changed the subject to, say, the Internet, he would have quickly headed back to the cheese tray.

Two years later, OJ Simpson still provided conversation, but was no longer the exclusive topic (my husband can even discuss the Internet now). When OJ was found "liable" in civil trial after he was found "not guilty" in the criminal trial, we had a dinner table debate over the semantics of guilt and innocence in English and French. I pointed out that one French official involved in the *affaire du sang*, (the scandal over government officials' knowledge of blood contaminated with AIDS virus that was used in transfusions), was deemed "*responsable*" but not "*coupable*," or, responsible but not guilty. "*Ce n'est pas la même chose*," he answered, still a true Frenchman.

What if there had been no OJ Simpson trial? I suppose my husband would have learned English anyway, but he would have been a wallflower at my office Christmas party.

Looking for Home

Elizabeth Weir

"Home is where the heart is," or so the saying goes, and having lived the last twenty years in the U.S.A. and become a citizen, I have never doubted that my true heart lies in some leafy suburb of my native England. But when I actually lived there during a recent five-month sabbatical, I found I did not quite belong as I had imagined. In spite of my thoroughly British accent, manners and dress, I bumbled like a foreigner.

Take, for example, my first foray to the shops in Headingly.

Jet-lagged, I strode along the busy main road, passing knots of uniformed girls walking home from school and women with laden baskets on their arms returning from the shops. Bicycles and small cars charged past, and packs of green double-decker buses bathed me in gusts of warm diesel breath; I inhaled grubby air, savored familiar smells and relished the sounds of English voices raised against the noise of traffic.

At the shops, I found a small supermarket where I had to ask fellow shoppers for advice about how I should prepare English cuts of meat such as "scrag end," "back end" and "undercut." The difference between streaky bacon and back bacon I could divine, and I rejoiced in finding Marmite, Bird's custard powder, spring greens, new potatoes, runner beans and Wensleydale cheese. Pleased with my purchases, I joined the queue waiting at the cramped checkout.

"Twenty-one pounds, sixty seven p.," the bored cashier told me when she had tallied my goods, and I began a close inspection of my bills and coins that had been lying idle in Minneapolis, waiting for this moment of re-use.

"I'm awfully sorry, but I forgot my glasses," I told the rock-faced cashier. "You'll have to tell me if this is a ten or a twenty pound note."

Her mascara-laden eyes flicked heavenward. "It's neither," she sighed. "It's a one pound, and it's out of date."

The long queue behind me began to shuffle its many feet and murmur at the delay.

"Are you telling me it's worthless?" I said, indignant that my cache of English money should be unusable.

" 'aven't taken 'em for years," she told me.

"And this?" I asked in my English voice, holding out a coin the size and weight of an American quarter. "Is this twenty-five pence?"

The cashier frowned. "It's ten p.," and she glanced over her shoulder to see where her supervisor stood, should this nutter become difficult.

The woman in the front of the queue took a step away from me, causing renewed shuffling behind her. But the queue was no longer restless; its attention was riveted on me. "There never 'as been no twenty-five p.," the cashier said, having successfully made eye contact with her supervisor.

"Where do you think she's been?" I heard the third woman in the queue ask the woman ahead of her.

"Look," I said, pulling two large mauve bills from my purse and holding out a palm full of coins to the cashier, "can you just take the twenty pounds, sixty-seven pence from this?"

With her supervisor closing in on us, the cashier took the two bills and picked among the coins, trying not to touch my hand.

"Sad, really, isn't it?" a droopy voice came from the queue.

When our transaction was completed, I shoved my shopping into plastic bags and hurried into the anonymity of the busy street. At a safe distance from the supermarket, I found a wooden bench, still damp from recent rain, and held my coins and bills at arm's length to read them and to understand their value before I ventured into Boots, the chemists. Letting my gaze extend beyond my fingers and what I now saw was a well-used, five pound note, I recognized one of the women from my queue nudging her companion and nodding in my direction. With acquired American directness, I caught the woman's eye, shrugged and smiled. She looked shocked, as though I had broken some rule, averted her eyes and scurried away.

And I continued to surprise others. After failing to find a familiar red pillar box for posting my letters, I tried to stuff my mail into a small slot outside the post office. "Won't get very far if you put them in there, love," an elderly man with a walking stick advised me. "That's for pensions. I'd put them in the proper box, if I were you," and he pointed with his stick to a wide-mouthed slot painted dark blue further along the wall.

Common terms that I should know as an Englishwoman foxed me, too. After being told I could buy clothes pegs in the "D.I.Y.," I was none-the-wiser than before I received this information. The D.I.Y. turned out to be a large, do-it-yourself hardware store, where a woman directed me to look for my pegs beyond the Strimmers.

Strimmers?

My dilemma is that England has changed during my long absence, and I have changed during my twenty years in the U.S.A.

And where do I belong, now? Where does my heart lie?

I am no longer quite so certain. I am an expatriate, that awkward transplant with roots in the soils of two countries.

My home is Minnesota. This I know. Yet, in the deep reaches of feeling, home is an idealized England, unchanged, endearingly familiar and present only in memory.

Plastic or Paper

Susan M. Tiberghien

"**P**lastic or paper, lady?" asked the young man with a pony tail, as I looked in my purse for enough cash to pay for the groceries.

It was summer vacation and I had returned to the States to become a new grandmother.

"May I pay with my American Express card?" I said to the woman at the register, not yet ready to tackle the option of plastic or paper.

"No, Ma'am, only Visa or Masters."

"And a check?"

"With two identification cards, Ma'am," she answered, handing me the stub. Her finger nails were extraordinary, longer than I remembered ever seeing and painted brilliant pink. "Do you have a driver's license?"

I started to fill out the check. "I have a driver's license but it's Swiss."

The young man who had asked me about plastic or paper eyed me with curiosity. He had three earrings of different lengths all on the same ear.

"What did you say dear?" asked the cashier.

The line behind me was getting longer, but it was also getting interested.

"I said my license is Swiss. I don't live here, I live in Switzerland."

Everyone turned toward me. If only I had a hint of a foreign accent, no one would have paid attention. This was Cambridge, Massachusetts, where in summertime one out of two people speaks a foreign language. But my English sounded like their English. Where did I come from? I looked American, I spoke American, but I didn't perform American.

"Let me see dear. I don't want to cause you trouble."

Appeasement.

"Plastic or paper, lady?"

Lady? I had learned from overseas that I was a woman in the States. What was this lady business? And ma'am? And dear?

"Honey, he just means how do you want it wrapped? In a plastic bag or in a paper bag."

I had such a large, attentive audience by now that I found the question difficult. Which was more ecological? I should give the right answer. Making paper bags destroyed the trees and forests. But was the plastic bio-whatever? I never had learned that word. I made a wish that the plastic be whatever it should be and said, "Plastic, please."

The young man seemed relieved. He snapped open a large bag and placed it on a frame at the end of the check-out counter. The plastic bag sat suspended.

"Your license please, and another piece of identity."

All this hassle for $22.20. I thought about giving the groceries back, but my daughter and French son-in-law were waiting for them - three tomatoes (they had asked me to look for organic ones), one romaine lettuce (not iceberg, but French and leafy), three red apples (they were so polished I squished one just a little to see if it was real), black olives (I hunted for them all over the store), sharp cheddar cheese (they didn't tell me there were a dozen varieties of sharp cheddar), and steak (ah, I thought, after thirty years in Europe I could easily choose steak, but no, there were meters - I mean yards - of packaged steaks, each with different names.) I couldn't give it all back; it was our dinner.

So out came my Swiss driver's license, written in French, with a photo of me about twenty years back, well, maybe thirty. The cashier looked again at me and then back at the photo. Skepticism. Next came my American passport, recently renewed, like one month ago. Mistrust. Grandmothers do age.

She rang for the manager, her bright pink nail poised on the bell.

I waited. The young man who was packing my groceries stopped and waited. The people in line stood still and waited. No one murmured, no one was impatient. This too was different. I could hear the air conditioners.

When the manager, dressed in a grey pin-stripe suit arrived, I was so confused I reached out to shake his hand. I was ready to apologize. I had only wanted to do the shopping for my daughter and son-in-law and their new baby, born three days earlier. I had flown from Geneva to be a grandmother. I was even trying to be an ecological grandmother.

"Is this all right?" I asked, pushing the check, the Swiss drivers' license, the American passport in his direction.

"Yes. Everything is fine." He smiled and wrote his signature on the back of my check. I felt a wave of general relief fall on me and my curious onlookers. "I always dreamed of going to Switzerland," he said.

Exit is the Object

Susan Rose

My friend Jan and I were playing this new game called *Expat Exit* the other day when we started arguing. We usually never argue but this was just too much for me to let pass. She was insisting that she could skip the language training, get good bargains at the flea market, and exit the game and get back home faster than I could.

"How can you get a bargain if all you can talk is English?!?" I demanded querulously. "They'll be laughing themselves dead behind your back."

Maybe I was really miffed because, unlike her, I had just chosen to take the language course and now had to sit out four turns.

She gave her superior little laugh-snort and reminded me that she's been abroad before, even if it was without spouse and children.

I stubbornly waited out my turns as she hit the antique market, decided to take a trip to the Costa del Sol, and ordered $395.00 worth of sportswear from L.L. Bean.

"Just because you got the company spouse," I grumbled, "still doesn't mean you can just do nothing but spend money the whole time."

I rolled a double five and had to decide if I'd teach English or work as a secretary for a branch of an American firm, neither of which I wanted to do. Jan rolled and went on another sight-seeing trip. I was green with envy and decided that my feelings about board games had remained intact since the time I used to have to play hours of *Candy Land* with my little sister. Then things started to change.

First, Jan had a child go to the hospital for oral surgery. She had to wait out two turns because the nurse didn't know anymore English than 'How are you.' Then, she couldn't argue about the bills with the insurance company and had to miss three more turns while she waited for her husband's secretary to come back from vacation to help them.

Meanwhile, I'd decided to give up baking altogether and moved ahead two turns because I didn't have to drive two hours to the American import store to get canned frosting and baking soda. On my next turn, I even decided to give up my American dentist and again got an extra two turns. Now we were neck and neck.

Jan rolled a double four and lost half of her moving allowance due to company cutbacks. Now what was she going to do with all those dumb antiques? I gloated.

I rolled a seven and had to decide between a two-year extension or moving to another country. Damn. Just as I was finally getting near the Exit. I took the extension.

Jan landed on the same square and went into a hissy fit. Personally I think she was sick of antiquing. She chose a new country and immediately installed her kids in the international school, ordered $989.45 worth of winter clothing from LandsEnd, and again chose to skip the language lessons.

I rolled a double six and got promoted to a two-person marketing division because I could speak English, fluently that is. But then I had to sit out a turn because my kindergartner had to repeat kindergarten at the local school. Whoever thought that one up? Still I was hopeful. I was only four squares away from the Exit and Jan was clearly behind.

But then she rolled a double five. Due to a sell-off, the company was closing its international division and she moved up to my square. My turn again. I picked up the dice and desperately exhaled on them as they sat in the palm of my hand, hoping to weight them with just enough vapor to get the number I needed to finish. I gently let them fall and opened my eyes: Double two! I was out the Exit and on my way home.

Now it was Jan's turn. She rolled, eyes shining with hope. It was near dinner time, we'd been playing this game much longer than we'd intended and we were both getting antsy and ready to quit.

"Four-baby, four-baby," she crooned and rolled. The dice fell from her opened fist, rolled two times, and landed clear as the little up-turned nose on her face: one up, each face.

She stared unbelievingly at the board and her destiny: INTERNATIONAL LIVING IS MORE THAN COLLECTING ANTIQUES. GO BACK TO SQUARE 4 AND LEARN A LANGUAGE.

She let out a high-pitched scream.

"There, there," I said, "it's only a game."

List of Authors

Susan Reynolds Baime (along with Victoria), is now back in the United States. In addition to being a writer and mother, Susan is also a wife, business consultant, college teacher, mistress of a black Labrador and keeper of a rose garden. She's studying French in hopes of another adventure abroad.

Sarah Colton left North Carolina in 1972 and has been wandering around Europe (mainly France) ever since. She accomplishes this with husband Pierre, daughters Elisabeth, Catherine and Florence, and dog Julietta. She still travels with the same small suitcase which she brought on her first trip to Europe. This provides the necessary illusion that her life is organized and portable, although instead of containing all of her possessions, it has become part of a (rather large) constellation of suitcases which accompanies her and her family. In various metamorphoses, the original suitcase has contained diapers, doll clothes, dog food, unadvisedly large amounts of cash, rare wine, baseball equipment, and the family silver. Sarah wishes she wrote more and wasted less time.

E. Niessen Davis is a writer who has published short stories in "little" magazines; she also writes poetry. After her book Silent Footfalls was published, she adapted it for Children's Theater and Mira Mesa College gave it a full production. The Davis family often traveled overseas as Ethel's husband was Controller for large projects under construction in South America, France, Spain, Germany and Turkey. "A wonderful life," she says. Now back home, she's working on her novel, Never Travel Without Children.

Erzsi Deak is an American writer who shares her Hungarian name with a celebrated werewolf. She lives in Paris with her Franco-American husband, Charles, and their three daughters, Zažou, Nelly and Yoyo, who all wince at her accent in French. She is President of the French chapter of the Society of Children's Book Writers and Illustrators and is currently at work on a young adult mystery novel.

Pat Duffy is a native New Yorker and she teaches writing and communication skills at the United Nations. Next to New York, her favorite places are Paris, Kunming and Taipei. Her article Taipei Tales was awarded a prize in the Literal Latte Travel Essay Contest. Other articles of hers have appeared in The Boston Globe, New York Newsday, The Village Voice and Ms Magazine. She is currently at work on a collection titled Travels, etc.

After finishing a degree in journalism at the University of Florida in Gainesville, **Debra Gawron** moved to France, married a Frenchman and stayed there for ten years. She was involved in all of the communication projects of WICE, a non-profit educational and cultural association, including text writing, brochure and catalog design and editing. She was active in the creative writing and literature departments of WICE and worked with the Paris Writers' Workshop. She worked in the marketing departments for the Walt Disney Company, both in Florida and in France, where she was also speechwriter for EuroDisney's President. Currently she operates her own public relations agency that represents Caribbean resorts and other tourist destinations.

Paula Gormly was born in New York and grew up in Tokyo, Hong Kong and Manila. A graduate of Wesleyan University and Teacher's College of Columbia University, she has worked in real estate, broadcasting and education, most recently as Director of TEFL for WICE, a non-profit educational and cultural association in Paris. She currently lives in Hong Kong with her husband and son, spending most of her time on the playground.

Monica Granqvist had already transformed her life from full-time mother (two sons and a daughter) to technical writer when, abruptly, she found herself uprooted from her native Sweden to Belgium. After two years in her adopted country, she's now starting to brace herself for the culture shock when she goes back.

Mary Hanford was born in Washington D.C. and raised in Europe and the American Southwest. She has traveled to Asia, Samoa, Australia, New Zealand, and Israel and taught in Mexico, Cameroon and Zimbabwe. She currently teaches English at Monmouth College in Illinois. Hanford has published poetry in numerous journals. Her poetry collection <u>Holding the Light</u> was published in 1991. Her latest articles and stories appear in <u>Echoes</u>, <u>Transitions Abroad</u> and <u>Wordplay</u> magazines. Hanford drifted to Italy, Ireland and England during recent school breaks. She expects her life will eventually wash up on a shore as a bottle filled with rough drafts.

Isabel Huggan is a Canadian writer with two collections of short stories to her credit - <u>The Elizabeth Stories</u> and <u>You Never Know</u> (both published and translated internationally). For the past ten years she has lived abroad, first in Kenya, then France, now the Philippines, because of her husband's work in agricultural development. She teaches graduate courses in creative writing at two universities in Manila, and in 1998 will be a Mentor in the Humber School of Writing program. She says adjustment to a new country is only funny after it's over.

Jan Kilner is a foreign service spouse who has lived in Turkey, France and East Berlin. With a Masters Degree in Nutrition her interest in food is professional as well as hedonistic. She was thrilled when the Berlin Wall fell but treasures her experience living there during the historically unique time that it was still standing. She and her husband have two children (the first born in Berlin). They have returned to Turkey where "Shopping for food is a delight!"

Camilla Lee has relocated eleven times in the thirty years of marriage to her husband. While most moves have centered somewhere between New York and Boston, she has lived overseas twice; in Hong Kong with two young sons, and later in Tokyo as empty nesters. She counts wonderful memories of each experience and has recently come to roost in Narragansett,

Rhode Island, home of her family's summer roots. Camilla won <u>Redbook</u>'s annual short fiction contest in 1984.

Constance Leisure is a writer and editor. She was formerly Books and Fiction Editor at <u>Family Circle Magazine</u> and then at <u>Ladies' Home Journal</u>. Her short stories have appeared in <u>Sun Dog</u>, <u>Paris Transcontinental</u> and <u>Ladies' Home Journal</u>. She lives in Paris with her husband and two children and a well brought-up fox terrier.

Leza Lowitz is an award-winning poet and fiction writer who lived in Tokyo for four years, writing for <u>Art in America</u>, <u>The Japanese Times</u> and others. Her books include translations of <u>Japanese women's</u> poetry, <u>A Long Rainy Season</u> and <u>Other Side River</u> (Stone Bridge, 1994 & 95) and art history, <u>Japan: Spirit and Form</u> (Tuttle, 1994). She has published a travel book, <u>Beautiful Japan</u> (Tuttle, 1996) and a volume of poetry, <u>Old Ways to Fold New Paper</u> (Wandering Mind, 1996).

Tara McKelvey has spent six years in Europe and South America. She is a freelance journalist and has written for *The* <u>New York Times</u>, <u>Mademoiselle</u>, <u>Entertainment Weekly</u> and other publications. She now lives in Poland with her husband and their two children.

After studying film at Wesleyan University, **Elizabeth Joseph-Mosely** returned to her hometown of Los Angeles to work in film development. In 1994, a brief sojourn in Paris turned into an indefinite stay when she unexpectedly fell in love with a Frenchman. Married in France, Elizabeth currently works for a French film company and is writing her first screenplay.

Ellen Newmark lived in Germany for seven years where she worked as an illustrator while the expatriate experience fueled her creative energies. Since returning to the United States in 1992, Ellen has worked as a writer and artist in southern California. She is the author of <u>Thyme Travel</u>, a book of essays and recipes from around the world. Still suffering from wanderlust, Ellen trekked through the rain forests of Costa Rica gathering material for her first novel.

Gisela Pacho has lived in Japan, Uganda and the United States. She is currently working toward a Master of Fine Arts in Fiction Writing through Bennington College in Bennington, Vermont.

Pamela Perraud, a native of Minneapolis, MN, has spent most of the last twenty years living abroad, mostly in France, but also in England and Brazil. A human resources professional, she has worked in various organizations overseas including IBM and the American Embassy in Paris. She was a founder of FOCUS Information Services in London and co-chaired the first WOMEN ON THE MOVE conference in Paris in 1990. Now based in New York City, she does cross-cultural and human resource consulting.

Marion Schmitz-Reiners worked her way around Germany as a journalist before crossing cultures in 1983 to settle with her Flemish husband in Antwerp, Belgium. She now freelances for various publications and, in 1994, wrote an autobiographical series of essays, <u>Der Fremde in meinem Bett</u> ("The Stranger in my Bed"), providing a fascinating insight into the nature of the Flemish culture.

Sandra L. Reid moved to London in 1984. While her husband pursued post-graduate studies, Sandra worked as an office temp, copy editor and reporter for AP-Dow Jones. In 1989, unable to persuade immigration officials to grant them residency, they settled in Washington State where Sandra is a full-time mom and part-time poet and writer.

Patricia Sanford Roberts is a freelance writer living in Brussels with her husband and younger daughter. Her articles focus mainly on gastronomy and she has spent the last ten years taste testing regional specialties from Ankara to Zeebrugge. After five years in Paris she is sure her body is made of one part red wine, two parts *crème fraiche*. She imagines she will eventually return to the home of Yankee pot roast but not before she has finished a thorough investigation of Belgian beer and chocolate.

Susan Lynn Rose traces her first realization that there was more to life than being popular back to when her parents pulled her out of the fourth grade to spend three months traveling throughout Greece in a VW van. Since then she has gravitated between Europe and the United States like the magnetic particles in an Etch-a-Sketch. After eight years in Switzerland, she is currently back on the Pacific Rim where she spent her childhood.

Patsy Souza, a seasoned expatriate, has lived in Canada, Bahrain, Saudi Arabia, Kuwait and England. Her living experiences have supplied ample material for short stories, and most recently, a one-act play. She twice attended the summer Art Workshop International in Assisi, Italy, where she participated in their writers' program. During her five years in Kuwait she formed a women's writing group and a mixed writing group. She continues to write and enjoy life abroad.

Susan M. Tiberghien, a writer from New York, married a Frenchman and moved to Europe thirty-five years ago. Her narrative essays appear in journals and anthologies in the U.S. and Europe, most recently Two Worlds Walking (New Rivers, '94), and Swaying (U of Iowa, '96). Author of Looking for Gold (Daimon Verlag, '95), she directs writers' workshops in the States and in Europe and currently lives in Switzerland where she edits the literary review, Offshoots, Writing from Geneva.

Drusilla Guérin Walsh has been on the move since 1950 when, under the auspices of the U.S. Navy she founded the Footlighter's Theater in Port Layautey, French Morocco. With her Parisian husband she lived in Iran, Kuwait, Holland, England and France. In Paris she directed the International Relocation Company and co-founded the New American Theater. She is the author of a novel placed in Iran and a collection of short stories.

Christa Weil's high school yearbook quotation read: "One never goes quite so far as when one doesn't know where one is going," which she feels is the perfect summation of life as an expat. Now living in London with her husband Dean, she is a freelance book editor for French and British publishers. She has written for various newspapers and magazines on the arts and culture, and is working on her first novel.

Elizabeth Weir grew up in England, worked as a nurse in South Africa and settled in Minnesota, U.S.A. with her husband and two sons, where she writes for a local newspaper, freelances and dabbles in poetry and prose.

Melanie Billings-Yun is a writer, lecturer and historian. She has lived in Hong Kong, Indonesia, Paris, London and is currently residing in Seoul where she directs a communications enterprise that teaches Korean business people American English and American customs/habits. Her husband is Korean, making their posting in Seoul a unique overseas assignment.

Publisher's Note:

I look at the computer screen and try to concentrate. As the cursor runs up and down the pages of the manuscript, I think 'what on earth am I trying to do?' Help women come to terms with cultural differences and the process of adjustment? I should know better...

When my daughter Nina announced she was getting married to a Romanian - who on top of it was illegal in Belgium - I flipped. Now is this destiny? Or is someone up there trying to teach me to be less smug and more human... pointing out that, even with the experience in cross-cultural living and work-ing that I have acquired over the last 30 years - I still have to adjust to a new situation like this.

I am so glad we settled for this title... it speaks right from the heart and vividly communicates the aches and pains that are only forgotten after a while - once the dust has settled.

Now, some weeks on, Nina and her beau have married in Romania and are sorting out their visas to come back to Belgium - and I will never forget the preparation of this book.

Karin Minke

Brussels, Belgium
September 1997

Europublications

WeEuropeans

Whatever doubts we may have about Maastricht, many of us hold fervently to the idea of a united Europe. And opinion polls among the young show a growing commitment to the European ideal.

This Europe is all about people – people who differ in their tastes and habits but share the same values and ideals. Understanding them, understanding one another, is a crucial step in the process of creating a Europe where unity cohabits with diversity.

Richard Hill talks about the people in this book. He starts by describing, then attacking, the stereotypes and moves on to a witty and skilful analysis of each of the European cultures.

He then enlarges his theme with a comparative analysis of value systems and lifestyles, how people communicate, relate to one another and do business. The final chapter examines recent events and offers thoughts on where we go from here.

"...a fascinating book. His dissection of each nationality produces some wonderful sociological insights."

The European

"Richard Hill starts from the obvious to discover the difficult and makes an impressive success of it."

Emanuele Gazzo, *Agence Europe*

"A delightful and very funny book. I'll buy it!"

Derek Jameson, *BBC Radio 2*

*"I can warmly recommend a wonderful book by Richard Hill, '**We**Europeans'."* **Libby Purves, *BA High Life***

"A delightful and very funny book. I'll buy it!"

Derek Jameson, BBC Radio 2

"One of the most interesting books I've ever looked at"

Patrick Middleton, Riviera Radio

"Das Buch 'Wir Europäer' des Engländers Richard Hill ist in Brüssel zum absoluten Bestseller avanciert. Mild ironisch analysiert er die Gewohnheiten der Euro-Völker, deckt Gemeinsamkeiten und Unterschiede auf, weist auf Stärken und Schwächen hin"

Birgit Svensson, Wochenpost

"Il fallait être Britannique pour oser le pari, il fallait avoir vécu longtemps à Bruxelles pour le réussir. C'est le cas de l'Anglais Richard Hill"

Violaine Muûls, L'Evénement

"'WeEuropeans' hoort verplichte lectuur te zijn voor elke deelnemer aan een Eurotop. Het zou de sfeer opvrolijken en de besluitvorming versnellen. De Europeanen, binnen en buiten de EG, zouden er wel bij varen. Om hen gaat het toch altijd, beweren de regeringsleiders onvermoeid"

Henk Aben, Algemeen Dagblad

"Wir Europäer: Zum Lachen!"

BZ am Sonntag

"Een onderhoudend boek, dat gezien de huidige ontwikkelingen binnen de Gemeenschap niet alleen actueel, maar ook leerzaam is"

Haye Thomas, Haagsche Courant

"I bästsäljaren 'We Europeans' finns vi redan med på ett hörn, som ett hyggligt men gammaldags folk med dörrar som öppnas utåt... 'We Europeans', en munter och innehållsrik bok som snabbt blivit populär bland EG-folket"

Dagens Nyheter, Sweden

"Hill mainitsee sivumennen myös, että suomalaiset juovat paljon. Tämäkin mielikuvaongelma jälleen kerran! Lukiessa eteenpäin käy ilmi, että hän tarkoittaa maidon kulutusta"

Turun Sanomat, Finland

EuroManagers
& Martians
Richard Hill

The Business Cultures of Europe's Trading Nations

EuroManagers & Martians

Looking at them simply as people, when we see them in the streets of Paris or when we visit them *chez eux*, our fellow-Europeans come across as a pretty odd lot – a far cry from the Single Market, harmonisation and all those dreary things.

But how do they behave in business? Put a German, a Frenchman, a Spaniard, an Italian, a Swede and, of course, a Brit together around a negotiating table and what happens? Either nothing at all – they just don't know how to deal with one another – or a lot! It's then that you realise that, despite all the constraints of working within a business environment, life à *l'européenne* is still full of surprises.

The simple fact, of course, is that it would need a superhuman to leave his cultural baggage behind him simply because he puts on his coat to go to the office. This book examines the business cultures of Europe's main trading nations and offers useful insights into differences in attitudes to time, hierarchy, protocol, negotiating styles, acceptance of management disciplines and multicultural teamwork.

With so much cultural diversity even in business, the author wonders how on earth we are going to develop the Euromanager we keep hearing about, the person who is going to save us from the Japanese, the Asian Tigers and others. Will this Euro-superman-ager ever exist?

"The book is written from an alien's point of view, and it presents both carefully researched and anecdotal evidence in an entertaining read... Carefully steering a course away from the stereotype path, Hill gives well-considered and practical advice on conducting Eurobusiness."　　　　**The European**

'The NewComers'

a book that 'takes the lid off'
the Austrians, Finns and Swedes

Many months after Austria's, Finland's and Sweden's accession to the European Union, ignorance about these countries is as great as ever.

Maybe not where they are, or what they represent economically, but who they are, how they do business, what things are important to them and what are not.

Now Richard Hill and David Haworth, a public affairs consultant specialising in the Nordic countries, have collaborated to write **"The NewComers"**.

This book sets out 'to take the lid off' the Austrians, Finns and Swedes, and explain them to their fellow-Europeans and others. The Norwegians were also supposed to be included but, sadly, things didn't work out that way.

"The NewComers" presents a family portrait of each of the three countries - their virtues, their quirks, tastes, habits and sensitivities, together with relevant background on history and politics.

This book provides even the most mildly curious with a clear and entertaining introduction to those who, from now on, will have a growing influence on the nature of the "new EU".

"I would like to congratulate you on this publication, which is not only a delightful read, but gives at the same time a very comprehensive insight into these countries, their people and mentalities"
Austrian Embassy Official

"Your style is extremely lucid and filled with tolerance and humour. May I inscribe myself in the Richard Hill and David Haworth fan club?" **Swedish lawyer and lobbyist**

"Delightful! You seem to have got the essence of this extremely complex society" **British businesswoman in Vienna**

GREAT BRITAIN LITTLE ENGLAND

Britons have recently been bombarded and bludgeoned with books examining the reasons for their country's dramatic decline.

But, while offering heavily documented analyses of culprit 'constituencies' - labour, management, educators, civil servants, government itself - these books have stopped short of examining the mindsets, motivations and mannerisms common to the actors in the drama.

In this book, Richard Hill sets out to fill the gap. Starting with himself, he tries to get under the skin of the British - more specifically, the English - and understand where they go right and why they go wrong.

This is an entertaining and thought-provoking book by a Briton who has had the advantage of living outside his island culture, yet consorting closely with it, for the last 30 years.

"I found it fascinating reading. If I weren't British (sorry, English), I would have enjoyed it."

Stanley Crossick,
The European Policy Centre

"Wonderful stuff. Witty and accurate without being cynical."
John Mole, author of 'Mind Your Manners'

"I am thoroughly enjoying reading it... it cheers up a Scottish Nationalist of a London evening!"

Margaret Ewing, MP

210

Have You Heard This One? An Anthology of European Jokes

Here are some of the better jokes we Europeans tell about one another. There are a lot of bad ones – far too many – but you will find none of them here.

Good European jokes are neither stupid nor abusive. They tell one something instructive about the way people from different cultures perceive one another. And some of these jokes shed light on the cultures of both the 'sender' and the 'receiver'.

Humour is the subtlest expression of culture, which explains why English people have difficulty in understanding German jokes. Even the psychology of humour is coloured by the attitudes of the different cultures. Yet there is common ground in European humour: some of these jokes turn up in various guises in various places.

As that eminent European Johann Wolfgang von Goethe said, rather severely: "There is nothing in which people more betray their character than in what they laugh at". Taken in the right spirit, humour is an excellent starting point for cross-cultural comprehension.

US & THEM

Author: Richard Hill
175 pages
format 195 × 130 mm (7 3/4 × 5")
ISBN 90-74440-10-X

**BEF 595   HFl 29,90   FF 90,-   £ 10.99   DM 34,-
AS 195   SFr 28,50   US$ 17.95**

In his new book, *Us & Them*, Richard Hill examines European separatism in its various forms: the regionalist movement, attitudes to minorities, the bonding instinct and, most significantly, the silent separatism that is now distancing the younger generations of Europeans from the world of politics.

Since his first book, *WeEuropeans*, came onto the market five years ago, Hill has had the opportunity to address audiences of students, undergraduates and graduates totalling over 6,000 young people of every European nationality.

In discussing European issues with them, he discovered that these young people have largely disengaged from conventional politics. They regard politicians with, at best, disinterest and, at worst, distaste or disrespect. This attitude is prevalent across all western European countries, with the possible exception of the Netherlands and Ireland.

Hill concludes: "The world has changed massively in the last fifty years, but western Europe still lives with the threat of social dislocation. Then, the problem was the divides that separated countries and cultures. Us was the mother-country, Them was the rest. Now, the dislocation is within countries and cultures, the growing gulf between Europe's young people and the society they were born into. Today Us is Europe's youth and Them is the rest of us".

Hill's conclusions are supported by the findings of national and international opinion studies, reviewed in detail in the book.

"I found this new book to be as exciting and witty as ever. I'll steal stuff from it if you don't mind, but will always give you credit!"

Gilles de Courtivron, Professor, McGregor School of Business, Ohio

"This is an astonishing book, not only because of the superbly lucid and vigorous writing, but also because the thoughts are equally rigorous and right in both form and substance. I have recommended it to my students."

Adelino Torres, Professor, Universidade Técnica de Lisboa

Europublic - An Open Door to Europe's Cultures

We publish and market books, provide
lecturers, organise training courses, all of them
devoted to one thing: the cultures of Europe.
Europublic author Richard Hill talks and lectures
regularly at the Centre for International Briefing,
the European Institute of Public Affairs, the
Helsinki Institute, and various European and
American universities and business schools.
For more details, ask for our catalogue
or visit our site on Internet:

http://www.understanding-europe.com

Order form

☐ **They Only Laughed Later**
ISBN 90-74440-12-6
BF 595 HFL 29.90 FF 90,- £10.99 DM 34,- AS 195,- SFR 28.50 US$ 17.95

☐ **Us & Them**
ISBN 90-74440-10-X
BF 595 HFL 29.90 FF 90,- £10.99 DM 34,- AS 195,- SFR 28.50 US$ 17.95

☐ **WeEuropeans**
ISBN 90-74440-05-3
BF 700 HFL 38.50 FF 115,- £13.99 DM 39.90 AS 215,- SFR 29.90 US$ 24.95

☐ **EuroManagers & Martians**
ISBN 90-74440-02-9
BF 695 HFL 38.50 FF 115,- £12.99 DM 39.90 AS 215,- SFR 29.90 US$ 20.95

☐ **Have You Heard This One? An Anthology of European Jokes**
ISBN 90-74440-08-8
BF 395 HFL 19.95 FF 65,- £ 5.95 DM 18.90 AS 135,- SFR 16.50 US$ 14.95

☐ **Great Britain, Little England**
ISBN 74-4440-04-5
BF 495 HFL 25.- FF 80,- £ 9.99 DM 29.90 AS 165,- SFR 24.90 US$ 15.95

☐ **The NewComers**
ISBN 90-74440-06-1
BF 595 HFL 29,90 FF 90,- £ 10.99 DM 34,- AS 195,- SFR 28,50 US$ 17.95

Please complete and fax to : +32-2-343.93.30
or send an e-mail to : kminke@europublic.com

Name : ....

Eurocard/Mastercard   ☐

Visa   ☐

Card N° : ....

Expiry Date : Month .... Year ....

Prices for bulk quantities on request.